VA

Paul-Eric Dumontier
François Rémillard
Pierre Longnus

ULYSSES
TRAVEL PUBLICATIONS
Travel better... enjoy more

Series Director
Claude Morneau

Project Supervisor
Pascale Couture

Research and Composition
Paul-Éric Dumontier
François Rémillard
Pierre Longnus

English Editors and Translation
Jennifer McMorran
Tracy Kendrick

Collaboration
Daniel Desjardins

Layout
Jennifer McMorran

Cartography
André Duchesne

Artistic Director
Patrick Farei
Atoll Direction

Illustrations
Lorette Pierson

Photography
Cover
Michel Gascon - Réflexion
Chapter Headings
Jennifer McMorran

Special Thanks: Ulysses Travel Publications would like to thank SODEC and the Canadian Heritage Ministry for their financial support.

Distributors

AUSTRALIA:
Little Hills Press
11/37-43 Alexander St.
Crows Nest NSW 2065
☎ (612) 437-6995
Fax: (612) 438-5762

GERMANY & AUSTRIA:
Brettschneider
Fernreisebedarf GmbH
Hauptstr. 5
85586 Poing bei
München
☎ 08121-71436
Fax: 08121-71419

NETHERLANDS:
Nilsson & Lamm
Pampuslaan 212-214
1380 AD Weesp (NL)
☎ 02940-65044
Fax: 02940-15054

SPAIN:
Altaïr
Balmes 69
E-08007 Barcelona
☎ (34-3) 323-3062
Fax: (3403) 451-2559

CANADA:
Ulysses Books & Maps
4176 Saint-Denis
Montréal, Québec
H2W 2M5
☎ (514) 843-9882,
ext.2232
Fax: 514-843-9448

GREAT BRITAIN AND
IRELAND:
World Leisure Marketing
9 Downing Road West
Meadows, Derby
UK DE21 6HA
☎ 1 332 343 332
Fax: 1 332 340 464

SCANDINAVIA:
Scanvik
Esplanaden 8B
Copenhagen K
DK-1263
☎ 33.12.77.66
Fax: 33.91.28.82

SWITZERLAND:
OLF
P.O. Box 1061
CH-1701 Fribourg
☎ 41.37.83.51.11
Fax: 41.37.26.63.60

BELGIUM:
Vander
Vrijwilligerlaan 321
B-1150 Brussel
☎ (02) 762 98 04
Fax: (02) 762 06 62

ITALY:
Edizioni del Riccio
Via di Soffiano 164 A
50143 Firenze
☎ (055) 71 63 50
Fax: (055) 71 33 33

SOUTH-EAST ASIA:
Graham Brash
32 Gul Drive
Singapore 2262
☎ 65.86.11.336
Fax: 65.86.14.815

U.S.A.:
Seven Hills Book
Distributors
49 Central Avenue
Cincinnati, Ohio, 45202
☎ 1-800-545-2005
Fax: (513) 381-0753

Other countries, contact Ulysses Books & Maps (Montréal), Fax : (514) 843-9448

"It has the combined excellence of Nature's gift and man's handiwork."

Stephen Leacock on Vancouver in
My Discovery of the West (1937)

TABLE OF CONTENTS

LIST OF MAPS

TABLE OF SYMBOLS

☎	Telephone number
⊷	Fax number
≡	Air conditioning
⊗	Ceiling fan
≈	Pool
ℜ	Restaurant
⊕	Whirlpool
ℝ	Refrigerator
K	Kitchenette
△	Sauna
☺	Exercise room
tv	Colour television
pb	Private bathroom
sb	Shared bathroom
ps	Private shower
½b	half-board (lodging + 2 meals)
bkfst	Breakfast

ATTRACTION CLASSIFICATION

★	Interesting
★★	Worth a visit
★★★	Not to be missed

HOTEL CLASSIFICATION

Unless otherwise indicated, the prices in the guide
are for one room in the high season,
double occupancy, not including taxes.

RESTAURANT CLASSIFICATION

$	$10 or less
$$	$10 to $20
$$$	$20 to $30
$$$$	$30 or more

Unless otherwise indicated, the prices in the guide are for a
meal for one person, including taxes, but not drinks and tip.

All prices in this guide are in Canadian dollars.

Canadian Cataloguing in Publication Data
Dumontier, Paul-Éric
     Vancouver
     (Ulysses travel guides)
     Translation of: Vancouver
     Includes index.
     ISBN 2-89464-014-5
1. Vancouver (B.C.) - Guidebooks. 2. Vancouver (B.C.) - Tours.
I. Rémillard, François. II. Longnus, Pierre.
III. Title. IV. Series.
FC3847.18.D8513 1996   917.11'33044   C96-940554-5
F1089.5.V22D8513 1996

Where is Vancouver?

British Columbia
Capital: Victoria
Language: English
Currency: Canadian dollar
Area: 950,000 km²

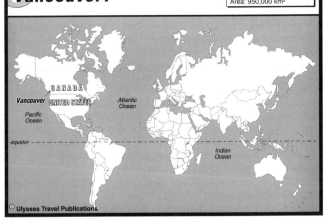

© Ulysses Travel Publications

PORTRAIT

Vancouver is truly a new city, one framed by the mighty elements of sea and mountains. As part of one of the most isolated reaches on the planet for many years, the city has over the last 100 years, developed close ties with the nations of the largest ocean on Earth, and is fast becoming the multicultural metropolis of the Pacific Rim. Although its history is closely linked to the development of British Columbia's natural resources, most residents were lured here by the magnificent setting and the climate, which is remarkably mild in a country known for its bitter winters and stifling summers. Vancouver, where Asia meets America, is a city well worth discovering.

Geography

Canada's Pacific coast, bounded by the 49th parallel to the south and the Alaskan border to the north, is dominated by the Coast Mountains, a group of peaks west of the Rockies, which form a barrier between the Pacific and the hinterland, a barrier broken in only a few places along the shoreline. The vast delta of the Fraser River proved suitable for human habitation, and it was there that Vancouver was founded. The city is now the third largest in Canada, with a population of nearly two million in the metropolitan area. It is also the only major city in the country that is decidedly turned toward the Pacific.

Contrary to what you might think, Vancouver does not actually face right onto the ocean, but is separated from the sea by Vancouver Island, where Victoria, the capital of British Columbia, is located. Vancouver, the province's economic hub, lies on the Strait of Georgia, an arm of the sea separating Vancouver Island from the mainland. Its population is scattered across two peninsulas formed by Burrard Inlet to the north and False Creek to the south.

Point Grey, the larger, more southerly peninsula, is home to the University of British Columbia and several sprawling residential neighbourhoods. On the smaller peninsula to the north, visitors will discover a striking contrast between the east end, with its cluster of downtown skyscrapers, and the west end, occupied by the lovely, unspoiled woodlands of Stanley Park. The circumscribed nature of this area, accessible by bridges and ferries, has led to a steady increase in the price of land in the centre and to major traffic problems for people who commute in to work from the city's suburbs and satellite towns. Finally, it is worth noting that Vancouver is only about 30 km from the U.S. border (and less than 200 km north of Seattle).

Vancouver boasts an exceptionally mild climate, with average temperatures of 3°C in January and 17°C in July. There is very little snowfall here during winter, though there is a lot of rain (annual average: 163 days of precipitation) and the summers are temperate and sunny. The westerly winds blow the clouds coming off the ocean into the Coast Mountains, causing heavy precipitation and generally very grey weather.

Plants thrive in this wet climate, and the wide variety of trees and flowers make Vancouver a vast, luxuriant garden. Not only are there species indigenous to the rain forest (the northern counterpart of the equatorial forest) like the enormous Douglas firs, red cedars, giant thujas, and western hemlocks but over the decades, countless European and Asian plants have been imported to satisfy the local residents' passion for gardening. The numerous private and public ornamental gardens in and around Vancouver are thus adorned with British, Canadian, Chinese and Japanese species, to name but a few.

History and Economic Development

■ Indigenous Peoples

Over 10,000 years ago, a number of tribes whose past melted away with the ice that once covered a large part of the northern hemisphere, travelled across the Bering Strait from Asia and scattered across North America, forming the numerous Amerindian nations and pre-Columbian civilizations of this continent. There is some doubt, however, as to whether native civilization on the West Coast originated with these vast waves of immigration. According to one theory, the ancestors of the West Coast tribes came here more recently (around 3000 B.C.) from various islands in the Pacific. Proponents of this hypothesis base their argument on the natives' art, traditions and spoken languages, which are not unlike those of the indigenous peoples of the Pacific archipelagos.

When the first whites arrived here in the late 18th century, the Vancouver region was inhabited by the Salish (the other speech communities on the Pacific coast are the Haida, the Tsimshian, the Tlingit, the Nootka-Kwakiutl and the Bellacoola). Like their compatriots, the Salish favoured this region for its remarkably mild climate and abundance of belugas, salmon, seals, fruit and other resources. This beneficial environment, combined with the barrier formed by the nearby mountains, enabled the coastal tribes to thrive. Not only was their population quite large, but it was also significantly denser than that of other native nations in central and eastern Canada.

In 1820, there were some 25,000 Salish living on the shores of the Fraser River, from its mouth south of Vancouver all the way up into the Rockies. Like other native tribes, the Salish were sedentary and lived in villages made up of red cedar longhouses. They traded with other natives along the coast during potlatches, festive ceremonies lasting weeks on end and marked by the exchange of gifts.

■ Belated Exploration

The 18th century saw an increase in exploration and colonization all over the world as European sea powers hungering for natural riches and new territories scoured the planet. The African shores were well charted, and no stone had been left unturned on the east coast of North America. There was, however, an immense area that still seemed inaccessible: the far-off and mysterious Pacific Ocean. Some of the many peoples inhabiting its shores were completely unknown to French, Spanish and English navigators. The Panama Canal had not yet been dug, and sailing ships had to cover incredible distances, their crews braving starvation, just to reach the largest of the Earth's oceans.

The voyages of French navigator Louis Antoine de Bougainville and English explorer James Cook, removed some of the mystery surrounding these distant lands. After Australia (1770) and New Zealand (1771), Cook explored the coast of British Columbia (1778). He did not, however, venture as far as the Strait of Georgia, where Vancouver now lies.

In 1792, Cook's compatriot George Vancouver (1757-1798) became the first European to trod upon the soil that would give rise to the future city. He was on a mission to take possession of the territory for the King of England, and by so doing put an end to any plans the Russians and Spaniards had of laying claim to the region. The former would have liked to extend their empire southward from Alaska, while the latter, firmly entrenched in California, were looking northward. Spanish explorers had even made a brief trip into Burrard Inlet in the 16th century. This far-flung region was not highly coveted enough to cause any bloody wars, however, and was left undeveloped for years to come.

The Vancouver region was not only hard to reach by sea, but also by land, with the virtually insurmountable obstacle of the Rocky Mountains blocking the way. Imagine setting out across the immense North American continent from Montreal, following the lakes and rivers of the Canadian Shield, and exhausting yourself crossing the endless Prairies, only to end up barred from the Pacific by a wall of rock several thousand metres high. In 1908, the fabulously wealthy fur merchant and adventurer Simon Fraser became the first person to reach the site of Vancouver from inland. This belated breakthrough had little impact on the region, though, since Fraser was unable to reach any trade agreements with the coastal tribes and quickly withdrew to his trading posts in the Rockies.

The Salish Indians thus continued to lead a peaceful existence here for many more years before being disrupted by white settlers. In 1808, except for sporadic visits by Russians, Spaniards and Englishmen looking to trade pelts for fabrics and objects from the Orient, the natives were still living according to the traditions handed down to them by their ancestors. In fact, European influence on their lifestyle remained negligible until the mid-19th century, at which point colonization of the territory began slowly.

■ **Development of Natural Resources**

In 1818, Great Britain and the United States created the condominium of Oregon, a vast fur-trading zone along the Pacific bounded by California to the south and Alaska to the north. In so doing, these two countries excluded the Russians and the Spanish from this region once and for all. The employees of the Northwest Company, founded in Montreal in 1784, combed the valley of the Fraser River in search of furs. Not only did they encounter the coastal Indians, whose precious resources they were depleting, but they also had to adapt to the tumultuous waterways of the Rockies, which made travelling by canoe nearly impossible. In 1827, after the Hudson's Bay Company took over the Northwest Company, a large fur-trading post was founded in Fort Langley, on the shores of the Fraser, some 90 km east of the present site of Vancouver, which would remain untouched for several more decades.

The 49th parallel was designated as the border between the United States and British North America in 1846, cutting the hunting territories in half and thereby putting a damper on the Hudson's Bay Company's activities in the region. It wasn't until the gold rush of 1858 that the region experienced another era of prosperity. When nuggets of the precious metal were discovered in the bed of the Fraser, upriver from Fort Langley, a frenzy broke out. In the space of two years, the valley of the golden river attracted thousands of prospectors, and makeshift wooden villages went up overnight. Some came from Eastern Canada, but most, including a large number of Chinese Americans, were from California.

In the end, however, it was contemporary industrialists' growing interest in the region's cedar and fir trees that led to the actual founding of Vancouver. In 1862, Sewell Prescott Moody, originally from Maine (U.S.A), opened the region's first sawmill at the far end of Burrard Inlet, and ensured its success by creating an entire town, known as Moodyville, around it. A second sawmill, called Hastings Mills, opened east of present-day Chinatown in 1865. Two years later, innkeeper Gassy Jack Deighton arrived in the area and set up a saloon near Hastings Mills, providing a place for sawmill workers to slake their thirst. Before long, various service establishments sprang up around the saloon, thus marking the birth of Gastown, later Vancouver's first neighbourhood.

In 1870, the colonial government of British Columbia renamed the nascent town Granville, after the Duke of Granville. The area continued to develop, and the city of Vancouver was officially founded in April 1886. It was renamed in honour of Captain George Vancouver, who made the first hydrographic surveys of the shores of the Strait of Georgia. Unfortunately, a few weeks later, a forest fire swept through the new town, wiping out everything in its way. In barely 20 minutes, Vancouver was reduced to ashes. In those difficult years, local residents were still cut off from the rest of the world, so the town was reconstructed with an eye on the long term. From that point on, Vancouver's buildings, whether of wood or brick, were made to last.

■ The Umbilical Cord

The end of the gold rush in 1865 lead to a number of economic problems for the colony of British Columbia. Due to American protectionism, local industrialists and merchants could not distribute their products in California, while Montreal was too far away and too hard to reach to be a lucrative market. The only favourable outlets, therefore, were the other British colonies on the Pacific, which paved the way for Vancouver's present prosperity. In 1871, British Columbia agreed to join the Canadian Confederation on the condition that a railway line linking it to the eastern part of the country be built.

Recognizing the potential of this gateway to the Pacific, a group of businessmen from Montreal set out to build a transcontinental railway in 1879. Angus, Allan, McIntyre, Strathcona (Smith), Stephen and the other men who joined forces under the Canadian Pacific banner were not thinking small; they wanted to transform Canada, theretofore only a nation in the political sense of the word, into an economically unified power. Canadian Pacific chose Port Moody (formerly Moodyville) as the western terminus of the railway. On July 4, 1886, the first train from Montreal reached Port Moody after a tortuous journey of about 5,000 km. British Columbia was no longer cut off from the rest of the world; from that point on, it was regularly supplied with goods from Europe, Quebec and Ontario, and could export its own raw materials to more lucrative markets.

A few years later, the tracks were extended 20 km to Vancouver in order to link the transcontinental railway to the new port and thereby allow greater access to the Asian market. This change proved momentous for the city, whose population exploded from 2,500 inhabitants in 1886 to over 120,000 in 1911! Many of the Chinese who had come to North America to help build the railroad settled in Vancouver when the project was finished, generating a certain degree of resentment among white residents, who found the new immigrants a little too exotic for their liking. Nevertheless, the Chinese who had worked for Canadian Pacific and the gold mines in the Rockies were soon joined by Asians from Canton, Japan and Tonkin. The city's Chinatown, which grew up between Gastown and Hastings Mills, eventually became the second largest in North America after San Francisco's.

At the beginning of the 20th century, the city's economic activity gradually shifted from Gastown to the Canadian Pacific Railway yards, located around Granville Street. Within a few years, lovely stone buildings housing banks and department stores sprang up in this area. Nevertheless, most local residents still earned their livelihood from the lumber and fishing industries, and lived in makeshift camps on the outskirts of town. In those days, therefore, downtown Vancouver's rapid development was to some extent artificial, based on visions of prosperity that would not be realized for some time yet. In 1913, the city was much like a gangling adolescent in the midst of a growth spurt. It was then that a major economic crisis occurred, putting an end to local optimism for a while. The opening of the Panama Canal (1914) and the end of World

War I enabled Vancouver to emerge from this morass, only to sink right back into it during the crash of 1929. During World War II, residents of Japanese descent were interned and their possessions confiscated. Paranoia prevailed over reason, and these second- and sometimes even third-generation Vancouverites were viewed as potential spies.

■ The New Metropolis of the Pacific

As a result of the Canadian Pacific railway company's strong presence on the West Coast, Vancouverites turned their attention away from the ocean stretched out before them and concentrated instead on their ties with central and eastern Canada. Nevertheless, the city's dual role as a gateway to the Pacific for North Americans and a gateway to America for Asians was already well established, as evidenced by the massive influx of Chinese immigrants from the 19th century onwards and the numerous import-export businesses dealing in silk, tea and porcelain. The name Vancouver has thus been familiar throughout the Pacific zone for over a century. Starting in 1960, a decline in rail transport to the east prompted the city to shift its attention outward and concentrate on its role as a Pacific metropolis.

With the explosive economic growth of places like Japan, Hong Kong, Taiwan, Singapore, the Philippines, Malaysia and Thailand, especially in regards to exportation, Vancouver's port expanded at lightning speed. Since 1980, it has been the busiest one in the country; 70.7 million tonnes of merchandise were handled here in 1991. Vancouver's pleasant climate and stunning scenery attract large numbers of eastern Canadians looking to improve their quality of life, as well as Asians seeking a new place to live and invest their money. For example, many affluent residents of Hong Kong, anxious about what might happen when their protectorate is returned to China in 1997, have chosen to relocate here.

Thanks to all this new blood, Vancouver (especially the downtown core) has enjoyed continued growth since the late 1960s. Even more than San Francisco or Los Angeles, Vancouver has a strong, positive image throughout the Pacific. It is viewed as a neutral territory offering a good yield on investments and a comfortable standard of living.

Population

Vancouver has always been considered the "end of the line" in Canada, the final destination for those looking for a better world. From the era of the steamship to that of the transcontinental railroad, and on to the modern age of the jumbo jet, the city has continued to attract adventurers eager to line their pockets, as well as more philosophical souls looking for peace and a sense of well-being. Located at the edge of a continent that developed from east to west, Vancouver was shrouded in mystery for many years, a sort of Eldorado tinged with Confucianism from the far reaches of the world. These two visions of Vancouver sometimes lead to confrontations between people concerned primarily with economics and developing natural resources and those more interested in ecology. In the end, though, everyone agrees and revels in Vancouver's west-coast way of life.

In 1989, there were 1,471,844 people living in Greater Vancouver; today, there are an estimated 1,720,000. The population has thus grown 14% over the past seven years, illustrating the city's economic vitality and the continued attraction it holds for newcomers. Even early on, Vancouver had a multi-ethnic population, but in the wake of the colonial era, residents of British descent still formed a large majority. A number of Americans came here during the gold rush, and soon after, the first wave of Chinese immigrants established the city's Chinatown, which grew considerably after the completion of the Canadian Pacific railway (1886), a good part of which was built by Asian labourers. Before long, a Japanese community was born, further diversifying the city's "Pacific" profile. Today, Vancouver has over 200,000 residents of Asian descent.

The city's cultural mosaic became that much richer in the 20th century, when immigrants from Europe (especially Germany, Poland, Italy and Greece) began arriving. In 1989, Vancouverites of British descent made up only about 30% of the total population. The French Canadian population, which has always been small in British Columbia, stands at about 29,000 (1986), while the native population has dwindled to 12,000 (1991).

Architecture

Vancouver was founded during an era of eager westward expansion. Within a few months in 1865, scores of wooden buildings sprang up here, providing the employees of the area's newly opened sawmills with places to sleep, purchase goods and entertain themselves. The vast majority of these makeshift structures fell victim either to the wear and tear of time or the devastating fire of 1886, which destroyed a large part of the young city. You can see one of the few buildings that has survived from that era in Pioneer Park (see p 87).

In the years following the fire, the centre of town, located in what is now Gastown, was reconstructed out of brick in order to prevent destruction of the growing city by another blaze. Although the earliest buildings of that era were modelled after the Italianate architecture that had enjoyed such great popularity on the east coast two decades prior (prominent cornices, small pediments over the doors and windows), Vancouver caught up quickly, adopting Richardson's neo-Romanesque style, as other cities all over North America had done. This style, inspired by French Romanesque art, was reinterpreted by Boston architect Henry Hobson Richardson, who designed massive, robust-looking structures with large, arched openings. Other late 19th-century buildings have more in common with the vernacular architecture of San Francisco (multi-level oriel windows overhanging the sidewalks, projecting cornices), evidence of Vancouver's close ties with the rest of the west coast.

At the beginning of the 20th century, Vancouver experienced a period of phenomenal growth. Entire neighbourhoods sprang up in a single summer. In most residential areas, wood was the material of choice, since it was inexpensive and available in large quantities. The risks of fire, furthermore, were minimal, as the houses were almost all free-standing. Space was not a problem, so San Francisco's Queen Anne style, characterized by numerous gables and turrets, was used for these homes. Downtown, brick slowly gave way to stone, a richer material, for proud Vancouverites were eager to show the rest of the world that they were dynamic and urbane. It is for that reason that the largest skyscraper in the British Empire (see Sun Tower, p 52) was built in Vancouver, rather than Toronto or

London, in 1912. Next, Canadian Pacific introduced the Château style to Vancouver, along with the Beaux-Arts style and its offshoots, neo-Classical revival and baroque revival, which are all well represented here. The Chinese community also made a significant contribution to the city's architecture, building narrow commercial buildings with deep loggias and parapets on top, reflecting an interesting blend of North American and Asian styles.

Starting in 1913, Vancouver experienced a growth slump, from which it did not truly recover until after the Second World War. Consequently, few new buildings went up in the twenties and thirties. You will nevertheless find a few examples of the Art Deco style here, including the Marine Building, which faces straight down West Hastings Street (see p 58) and is viewed as one of the landmarks of the business district.

As Vancouver is a thriving young city, its architecture is predominantly modern and post-modern. Thanks to talented architects who are open to experimentation and a cultural climate that combines innovative Californian influences with the traditional building techniques of China, Japan and even some of British Columbia's native communities, the city has developed an exceptional and modern architectural heritage since the 1940s.

From the glass and steel skyscrapers downtown to the houses clinging to the mountainside in North and West Vancouver, with their simple post-and-beam construction, the accent is usually on purity of line. This sober, sophisticated style contrasts sharply with the ostentation of the early part of the century... and to a certain extent that of contemporary, late 20th-century architecture as well. Indeed, since the emergence of post-modernism, there has been a shift back to the lavish forms of the past. Many recent immigrants favour columns and decorated pediments, which they proudly photograph for their families back home. In some areas, furthermore, houses built in the fifties and sixties are being replaced by what Vancouverites have termed Monsterhouses, giant structures that take up almost their entire plot of land, usurping space once occupied by trees and gardens.

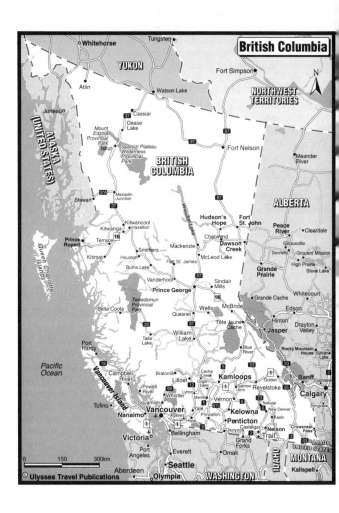

British Columbia

Whitehorse Tungsten
YUKON Fort Simpson
Atlin Watson Lake NORTHWEST TERRITORIES
Juneau Cassier
ALASKA (UNITED STATES) Mount Edzina Provincial Park Dease Lake
Iskut Fort Nelson
Spatsizi Plateau Wilderness Provincial Park BRITISH COLUMBIA Meander River
Stewart Meziadin Junction
Kitwancool Hazelton Hudson's Hope Fort St. John ALBERTA
Prince Rupert Kitwanga Terrace Chetwynd Peace River Cleardale
Smithers Mackenzie Dawson Creek Girouxville
Kitimat Houston McLeod Lake Donnelly Groundbirch Mission
Burns Lake Fort St. James High Prairie Slave Lake
Queen Charlotte Islands Vanderhoof Sinclair Mills Grande Prairie
Prince George Whitecourt
Tweedsmuir Provincial Park Wells McBride Grande Cache
Bella Coola Quesnel Edson
Tête Jaune Cache Hinton Drayton Valley
William Lake Jasper
Talla Lake Blue River Rocky Mountain House Sylvan Lake
Port Hardy
Pacific Ocean Campbell River Bralorne Cache Creek Logan Lake Kamloops Salmon Arm Golden Banff Cochrane
Lillooet Revelstoke
Powell River Lytton Merritt Vernon Nakusp Calgary
Whistler Yale Kelowna New Denver Longview
Tofino Squamish Agassiz Princeton Penticton Kaslo
Nanaimo Vancouver Hope Castlegar Nelson
Victoria Bellingham Osoyoos Grand Forks Trail Crowsnest Pass
Port Angeles Omak CANADA UNITED STATES
Everett IDAHO MONTANA
0 150 300km Aberdeen Seattle Kalispell
© Ulysses Travel Publications Olympia WASHINGTON

PRACTICAL INFORMATION

I nformation in this chapter will help visitors better plan their trip to Vancouver.

Entrance Formalities

■ Passport

For a stay of less than three months in Canada, a valid passport is usually sufficient for most visitors and a visa is not required. American residents do not need a passport, though it is the best form of identification. A three-month extension is possible, but a return ticket and proof of sufficient funds to cover this extension may be required.

Caution: some countries do not have an agreement with Canada concerning health and accident insurance, so it is advisable to have the appropriate coverage. For more information, see the section entitled **"Health"** on page 40.

Canadian citizens who wish to enter the United States do not need a visa, neither do citizens from the majority of Western European countries. A valid passport is sufficient for a stay of less than three months. A return ticket and proof of sufficient funds to cover your stay may be required.

■ Extended Visits

Visitors must submit a request to extend their visit **in writing** and **before** the expiration of their visa (the date is usually written in your passport) to an Immigration Canada office. To make a request you must have a valid passport, a return ticket, proof of sufficient funds to cover the stay, as well as the $65 non-refundable filing-fee. In some cases (work, study), however, the request must be made **before** arriving in Canada.

Customs

If you are bringing gifts into Canada, remember that certain restrictions apply.

Smokers (minimum age is 16) can bring in a maximum of 200 cigarettes, 50 cigars, 400 g of tobacco, or 400 tobacco sticks.

For wine and alcohol the limit is 1.1 litres; in practice, however, two bottles per person are usually allowed. The limit for beer is 24 355-ml size cans or bottles.

Plants, vegetation, and food: there are very strict rules regarding the importation of plants, flowers, and other vegetation; it is therefore not advisable to bring any of these types of products into the country. If it is absolutely necessary, contact the Customs-Agriculture service of the Canadian embassy **before** leaving.

Pets: if you are travelling with your pet, you will need a health certificate (available from your veterinarian) as well as a rabies vaccination certificate. It is important to remember that the vaccination must have been administered **at least** 30 days **before** your departure and should not be more than a year old.

Tax reimbursements for visitors: it is possible to be reimbursed for certain taxes paid on purchases made while in Western Canada (see p 43).

Embassies and Consulates

■ Abroad

Australia
Canadian Consulate General
Level 5, Quay West
111 Harrington Road
Sydney, N.S.W.
Australia 2000
☎ (612) 364-3000
⌨ (612) 364-3098

Belgium
Canadian Embassy
2 Avenue de Tervueren
1040 Brussels
☎ 735.60.40
⌨ 732.67.90

Denmark
Canadian Embassy
Kr. Bernikowsgade 1,
DK = 1105 Copenhagen K,
Denmark
☎ 12.22.99
⌨ 14.05.85

Finland
Canadian Embassy
Pohjos Esplanadi 25 B,
00100 Helsinki, Finland
☎ 171-141
⌨ 601-060

Germany
Canadian Consulate General
Internationales
Handelzentrum
Friedrichstrasse 95, 23rd
Floor
10117 Berlin, Germany
☎ 261.11.61
⌨ 262.92.06

Great Britain
Canada High Commission
Macdonald House
One Grosvenor Square
London W1X 0AB
England
☎ 258-6600
⌨ 258-6384

Netherlands
Canadian Embassy
Parkstraat 25
2514JD The Hague
Netherlands
☎ 361-4111
⌨ 365-6283

Norway
Canadian Embassy
Oscars Gate 20,
Oslo 3, Norway
☎ 46.69.55
⌨ 69.34.67

Sweden
Canadian Embassy
Tegelbacken 4, 7th floor,
Stockholm, Sweden
☎ 613-9900
⌨ 24.24.91

Switzerland
Canadian Embassy
Kirchenfeldstrasse 88
3000 Berne 6
☎ 532.63.81
✉ 352.73.15

United States
Canadian Embassy
501 Pennsylvania Avenue,
N.W.
Washington, DC
20001
☎ (202) 682-1740
✉ (202) 682-7726

Canadian Consulate General
Suite 400 South Tower
One CNN Center
Atlanta, Georgia
30303-2705
☎ (404)   577-6810   or
577-1512
✉ (404) 524-5046

Canadian Consulate General
Three Copley Place
Suite 400
Boston, Massachusetts
02116
☎ (617) 262-3760
✉ (617) 262-3415

Canadian Consulate General
Two Prudential Plaza
180 N. Stetson Avenue,
Suite 2400,
Chicago, Illinois
60601
☎ (312) 616-1860
✉ (312) 616-1877

Canadian Consulate General
St. Paul Place, Suite 1700
750 N. St. Paul Street
Dallas, Texas
75201
☎ (214) 922-9806
✉ (214) 922-9815

Canadian Consulate General
600 Renaissance Center
Suite 1100
Detroit, Michigan
48234-1798
☎ (313) 567-2085
✉ (313) 567-2164

Canadian Consulate General
300 South Grande Avenue
10th Floor, California Plaza
Los Angeles, California
90071
☎ (213) 687-7432
✉ (213) 620-8827

Canadian Consulate General
Suite 900, 701 Fourth
Avenue South
Minneapolis, Minnesota
55415-1899
☎ (612) 333-4641
✉ (612) 332-4061

Canadian Consulate General
1251 Avenue of the
Americas
New York, New York
10020-1175
☎ (212) 596-1600
✉ (212) 596-1793

Canadian Consulate General
One Marine Midland Center
Suite 3000
Buffalo, New York
14203-2884
☎ (716) 852-1247
✺ (716) 852-4340

Canadian Consulate General
412 Plaza 600
Sixth and Stewart Streets
Seattle, Washington
98101-1286
☎ (206) 442-1777
✺ (206) 443-1782

■ **In Vancouver**

Australian Consulate
999 Canada Place
Suite 602
Vancouver, BC
V6C 3E1
☎ (604) 684-1177

Consulate General of the Netherlands
475 Howe Street
Suite 821
Vancouver, BC
V6C 2B3
☎ (604) 684-6448

Honorary Consulate of Belgium
Birks Place
Suite 570
688 West Hastings
Vancouver, BC
V6B 1P4
☎ (604) 684-6838

Consulate General of Switzerland
999 Canada Place
Suite 790
Vancouver, BC
V6C 3E1
☎ (604) 684-2231

British Consulate General
111 Melville St.
Suite 800
Vancouver, BC
V6E 3V6
☎ (604) 683-4421

U.S. Consulate General
1095 West Pender
Vancouver, BC
V6E 2M6
☎ (604) 685-4311

Consulate General of Germany
World Trade Centre
999 Canada Place
Suite 704
Vancouver, BC
V6C 3E1
☎ (604) 684-8377

Tourist Information

The **Vancouver TouristInfo Centre** *(May to Sep, every day 8am to 6pm; Sep to May, Mon to Fri 8:20am to 5pm, Sat 9am to 5pm; Plaza Level, Waterfront Centre, 200 Burrard St., ☎ 682-2222, 683-2000 or 1-800-888-8835)* provides information on sights and accommodations.

Internet:
http://www.city.net/countries/canada/british_columbia/

 Finding Your Way Around

■ **By Plane**

From Europe

There are two possibilities: direct flights or flights with a stop over in Montreal, Toronto or Calgary. Direct flights are of course much more attractive since they are considerably faster than flights with a stopover (for example expect about nine hours from Amsterdam for a direct flight compared to 13 hours). In some cases, however, particularly if you have a lot of time, it can be advantageous to combine a charter flight from Europe with one of the many charter flights within Canada from either Montreal or Toronto. Prices for this option can vary considerably depending on whether you are travelling during high or low season.

At press time, five airline companies offered direct flights from Europe to Vancouver.

From Europe

Air Canada offers daily direct flights during the summer from Paris to Vancouver and from London to Vancouver. Air Canada also flies twice a week from Frankfurt to Vancouver.
Canadian Airlines offers direct flights from London to Vancouver, as well as direct flights from Frankfurt to Vancouver.

KLM offers a direct flight from Amsterdam to Vancouver three times a week.

Lufthansa offers a daily flight in partnership with Canadian Airlines from Frankfurt to Vancouver.

British Airways offers daily non-stop service from London to Vancouver.

From the United States

Travellers arriving from the southern or southeastern United States may want to consider **American Airlines** which flies into Vancouver through Dallas.

Delta Airlines offers direct flights from Los Angeles to Vancouver. Travellers from the eastern United States go through Salt Lake City.

Northwest Airlines flies into Vancouver via Minneapolis.

From Asia

Both **Air Canada** and **Canadian Airlines** offer direct flights between Vancouver and Hong Kong.

Within Canada

Air Canada and **Canadian Airlines** are the only companies that offer regular flights to Vancouver within Canada. Daily flights to Vancouver as well as many other cities are offered from all the major cities in the country. Flights from Eastern Canada often have stop-overs in Montreal or Toronto. For example Air Canada flies to Vancouver 14 times a week. During the high season, the aforementioned flights are complemented by many others offered by charter companies, including Air Transat, Royal and Canada 3000. These flights are subject to change with respect to availability and fares.

Air Canada's regional partner **Air BC** offers flights within British Columbia, as does Canadian Airlines' regional partner, **Canadian Regional**.

■ Airport

Vancouver International Airport *(☎ 276-6101)* is served by flights from across Canada, the United States, Europe and Asia. Nineteen airline companies presently use the airport. The airport is located 15 km from downtown. It takes about 30 minutes to get downtown by car or bus. A taxi or limousine will cost you about $30, or you can take the **Airport Express Bus** *(☎ 270-4442)* which offers shuttle service to the major downtown hotels. This costs $9 per person.

Take note: even if you have already paid various taxes included in the purchase price of your ticket, Vancouver International Airport charges every passenger an **Airport Improvement Fee** (AIF). The fee is $5 for flights within B.C., $10 for flights elsewhere in North America, and $15 for overseas flights; credit cards are accepted, and most in-transit passengers are exempted.

Besides the regular airport services (duty-free shops, cafeterias, restaurants, etc.) you will also find an exchange office. Several car rental companies also have offices in the airport, including Avis, Thrifty, ABC Rent-a-Car, Budget (see p 33).

■ By Train

Travellers with a lot of time may want to consider the train, one of the most pleasant and impressive ways to discover Western Canada and reach Vancouver. Via Rail Canada is the only company that offers train travel between the Canadian provinces. This mode of transportation can be combined with air travel (various packages are offered by Air Canada and Canadian Airlines) or on its own from big cities in Eastern Canada like Toronto or Montreal. This last option does require a lot of time however, it takes a minimum of five days to get from Montreal to Vancouver.

The **CanRailpass** is another particularly interesting option. Besides the advantageous price, you only need to purchase one ticket for travel throughout Canada. The ticket allows 12 days of unlimited travel in a 30-day period. At press-time the CanRailpass was $572 in the high season and $390 in the low season. CanRailpass holders are also entitled to special rates for car rentals.

Via Rail offers several discounts:

Reductions for certain days of the week, during the off-season and on reservations made at least five days in advance: up to 40% off depending on the destination;

Discount for students and those 24 years of age or less: 10% throughout the year or 40% if the reservation is made five days in advance, except during the holidays;

Discount for people aged 60 and over: 10% on certain days during off-peak travel times;

Special rates for children: children two to 11 travel for half-price; children under two accompanied by an adult travel free;

Finally, take note that first-class service is quite exceptional, including a meal, wine, and alcoholic beverages free of charge.

For further information on Via Trains:

In Canada: ☎ 1-800-561-8630 or contact your travel agent
In the United States: ☎ 1-800-561-3949 or contact Amtrak or your travel agent
In Europe: in the United Kingdom contact Long-Haul Leisurail at ☎ 0733-335-599 or by fax at 0733-505-451, or Airsavers at ☎ 041-303-0308 or by fax at 041-303-0306. Express Conseil in Paris ☎ 44.77.87.94 can also book Via tickets.
Internet: http://www.viarail.ca

Trains from the United States and Eastern Canada arrive at the new intermodal **Pacific Central Station** *(Via Rail Canada, 1150 Station St.,* ☎ *1-800-561-8630)* where you can also connect to buses or the surface public transportation system known as the **Skytrain**. The cross-country Via train, **The Canadian** arrives in Vancouver three times a week from Eastern

Canada. The trip from Edmonton to Vancouver is a spectacular trip through the mountains along the rivers and valleys. Those in a rush should keep in mind that the trip takes 24 hours, and is more of a tourist excursion than a means of transportation. It costs less that $200 one-way; check with Via, however about seasonal rates.

BC Rail *(1311 West First St., North Vancouver, ☎ 984-5246)* trains travel the northern west coast. Schedules vary depending on the seasons.

During the summer, the **Great Canadian Railtour Company Ltd.** offers **Rocky Mountain Railtours** *($620 per person, $565 per person double occupancy; ☎ 606-7200 or 1-800-665-7245, ≈ 606-7520)* between Calgary and Vancouver.

■ **By Ferry**

Two ferry ports serve the greater Vancouver area for travellers coming from other regions in the province. Horseshoe Bay to the west and Tsawwassen to the south, are both about 30 min from downtown. For information contact the **British Columbia Ferry Corporation BC Ferry** *(☎ 277-0277 or 669-1211)*.

■ **By Bus**

The new intermodal **Pacific Central Station** was opened in 1993 in the old Via Station to allow travellers to connect between bus, train and public transportation in one place. Buses provide several links with the main cities in the province.

Greyhound Lines of Canada: Pacific Central Station, 1150 Station St., ☎ 662-3222 or 1-800-661-8747.

■ **By Car**

Vancouver is accessible by the TransCanada Highway 1, which runs east-west. This national highway links all of the major Canadian cities. It has no tolls and passes through some spectacular scenery. Coming from Alberta you will pass through the Rocky Mountains, desert regions and a breathtaking canyon. It is 975 km from Calgary, Alberta to Vancouver.

The city is generally reached from the east by taking the "Downtown" exit from the TransCanada. If you are coming from the United States or from Victoria by ferry, you will enter the city on Highway 99 North; in this case expect about 30 min to reach downtown.

Driver's licenses from Western European countries are valid in Canada and the United States. While North American travellers won't have any trouble adapting to the rules of the road in Western Canada, European travellers may need a bit more time to get used to things. Here are a few hints:

Pedestrians: Drivers in Western Canada are particularly courteous when it comes to pedestrians, and willingly stop to give them the right of way even in the big cities, so be careful when and where you step off the curb. Pedestrian crosswalks are usually indicated by a yellow sign. When driving pay special attention that there is no one about to cross near these signs.

Turning **right on a red light** when the way is clear is permitted in British Columbia.

When a **school bus** (usually yellow in colour) has stopped and has its signals flashing, you must come to a complete stop, no matter what direction you are travelling in. Failing to stop at the flashing signals is considered a serious offense, and carries a heavy penalty.

Wearing of **seatbelts** in the front and back seats is mandatory at all times.

Almost all highways in Western Canada are toll-free, and just a few bridges have tolls. The **speed limit** on highways is 100 km/h. The speed limit on secondary highways is 90 km/h, and 50 km/h in urban areas.

Gas Stations: Because Canada produces its own crude oil, gasoline prices are much less expensive than in Europe, and only slightly more than in the United States. Some gas stations (especially in the downtown areas) might ask for payment in advance as a security measure, especially after 11pm.

Driving in the City

Getting around Vancouver by car is easy; take note, however, that government has decided not to build any expressways through downtown, which is exceptional for a city of 1.7 million people; as a result rush-hour traffic can be quite heavy. If you have the time, by all means explore the city on foot.

Car Rentals

Packages including air travel, hotel and car rental or just hotel and car rental are often less expensive than car rental alone. It is best to shop around. Remember also that some companies offer corporate rates and discounts to auto-club members. Some travel agencies work with major car rental companies (Avis, Budget, Hertz, etc.) and offer good values; contracts often include added bonuses (reduced ticket prices for shows, etc.).

When renting a car, find out if the contract includes unlimited kilometres, and if the insurance provides full coverage (accident, property damage, hospital costs for you and passengers, theft).

Certain credit cards, gold cards for example, cover the collision and theft insurance. Check with your credit card company before renting.

To rent a car you must be at least 21 years of age and have had a driver's license for **at least** one year. If you are between 21 and 25, certain companies (for example Avis, Thrifty, Budget) will ask for a $500 deposit, and in some cases they will also charge an extra sum for each day you rent the car. These conditions do not apply for those over 25 years of age.

A credit card is extremely useful for the deposit to avoid tying up large sums of money.

Most rental cars come with an automatic transmission, however you can request a car with a manual shift.

Child safety seats cost extra.

Car Rental Companies

You can rent a car at the airport or in the city.

Downtown:

Tilden: 1140 Alberni St., ☎ 685-6111
Budget: 450 West Georgia, ☎ 668-7000
ABC Rent-a-Car: 1133 West Hastings, ☎ 681-8555 or 1-800-464-6422
Thrifty: 1400 Robson St., ☎ 276-0816
Avis: ☎ 689-2847

Accidents and Emergencies

In case of serious accident, fire or other emergency dial ☎ **911** or **0**.

If you run into trouble on the highway, pull onto the shoulder of the road and turn the hazard lights on. If it is a rental car, contact the rental company as soon as possible. Always file an accident report. If a disagreement arises over who was at fault in an accident, ask for police help.

■ By Taxi

Hailing a taxi in Vancouver is not a problem, especially near the entrances of the big downtown hotels and along main arteries such as Robson Street and Georgia Street. The main taxi companies are:

Yellow Cab *(☎ 681-1111)*
McLure's *(☎ 731-9211)*
Black Top *(☎ 731-1111)*

■ Public Transportation

BC Transit bus route maps are available from the Vancouver Travel InfoCentre *(summer, every day 8am to 6pm; rest of the year, Mon to Fri 8:30am to 5pm, Sat 9am to 5pm; 200 Burrard Street, ☎ 683-2000)*.

Vancouver has a rail transit system called the **Skytrain**, running east from the downtown area to Burnaby, New Westminster and Surrey. These automatic trains run from 5am to 1am all week, except Sundays when they start at 9am. The **Seabus**, a marine bus in the form of a catamaran, shuttles frequently between Burrard Inlet and North Vancouver.

Tickets and passes are available for **BC Transit**, the Skytrain and Seabus from the coin-operated machines at some stops, in some convenience stores or by calling ☎ 261-5100.

The fares are the same whether you are travelling on a BC Transit bus, the Skytrain or the Seabus. A single ticket generally costs $1.50, except at peak hours (in the morning before 9am and from 3pm to 6:30pm) when the system is divided into three zones and it costs $1.50 for travel within one zone, $2.25 within two zones and $3 within three zones.

■ **Handicapped Transportation**

Handydart *(300-3200 East 54th St.,* ☎ *430-2692)* provides public transportation for wheelchair-bound individuals. You must reserve your seat in advance.

Vancouver Taxis *(2205 Main St.,* ☎ *255-5111 or 874-5111)* also offers transportation for handicapped individuals.

■ **On Foot**

The best way to truly appreciate the many facets of any city is generally by foot. This guide outlines nine walking tours in different neighbourhoods. Don't forget your walking shoes!

Time Difference

Vancouver is in the Pacific time zone. It is therefore 3 hours behind Montreal and New York, eight hours behind the United Kingdom and nine hours behind continental Europe. Daylight Savings Time (+ 1 hour) begins the first Sunday in April and ends on the last Sunday in October.

Business Hours and Public Holidays

■ Business Hours

Stores

Generally stores remain open the following hours:

Mon to Fri	10am to 6pm;
Thu and Fri	10am to 9pm;
Sat	9 am or 10am to 5pm;
Sun	noon to 5pm

Well-stocked convenience stores that sell food are found throughout Western Canada and are open later, sometimes 24 hours a day.

Banks

Banks are open Monday to Friday from 10am to 3pm. Most are open on Thursdays and Fridays, until 6pm or even 8pm. Automatic teller machines are widely available and are open night and day.

Post Offices

Large post offices are open Monday to Friday from 9am to 5pm. There are also several smaller post offices located in shopping malls, convenience stores, and even pharmacies; these post offices are open much later than the larger ones.

■ Holidays and Public Holidays

The following is a list of public holidays in the province of British Columbia. Most administrative offices and banks are closed on these days.

January 1 and 2
Easter Monday and or Good Friday
Victoria Day: the 3rd Monday in May
Canada Day: July 1st
Civic holiday: 1st Monday in August
Labour Day: 1st Monday in September
Thanksgiving: 2nd Monday in October
Remembrance Day: November 1 (only banks and federal government services are closed)
Christmas Day: December 25

Mail and Telecommunications

■ Mail

Canada Post provides efficient (depending on who you talk to) mail service across the country. At press time, it cost 45¢ to send a letter elsewhere in Canada, 50¢ to the United States and 90¢ overseas. Stamps can be purchased at post offices and in many pharmacies and convenience stores.

■ Telecommunications

At press time the area code for Vancouver and the province of British Columbia was ☎ 604. BC Tel does, however, have plans to change this in the fall of 1996. The lower mainland and Vancouver and area will keep the ☎ 604 area code, while the area code for Vancouver Island, eastern, central and northern British Columbia will become ☎ 250.

Long distance charges are cheaper than in Europe, but more expensive than in the U.S.. Pay phones can be found everywhere, often in the entrance of larger department stores, and in restaurants. They are easy to use and most accept credit cards. Local calls to the surrounding areas cost $0.25 for unlimited time. Have a lot quarters on hand if you are making a long distance call. It is less expensive to call from a private residence. 1-800 and 1-888 numbers are toll free.

BC Tel sells phone cards in various denominations for use in pay phones to place local and long distance calls.

Money and Banking

■ Exchange

Most banks readily exchange American and European currencies but almost all will charge **commission**. There are, however, exchange offices that do not charge commissions and have longer hours. Just remember to **ask about fees** and **to compare rates**.

Traveller's Cheques

Traveller's cheques are accepted in most large stores and hotels, however it is easier and to your advantage to change your cheques at an exchange office. For a better exchange rate buy your traveller's cheques in Canadian dollars before leaving.

Credit Cards

Most major credit cards are accepted at stores, restaurants and hotels. While the main advantage of credit cards is that they allow visitors to avoid carrying large sums of money, using a credit card also makes leaving a deposit for car rental much easier and some cards, gold cards for example, automatically insure you when you rent a car (check with your credit card company to see what coverage it provides). In addition, the exchange rate with a credit card is generally better. The most commonly accepted credit cards are Visa, MasterCard, and American Express.

■ Banks

Banks can be found almost everywhere and most offer the standard services to tourists. Visitors who choose to stay in Canada for a long period of time should note that **non-residents** cannot open bank accounts. If this is the case, the best way to have money readily available is to use traveller's cheques. Withdrawing money from foreign accounts is expensive. However, several automatic teller machines accept foreign bank cards, so that you can withdraw directly from your account. Money

CANADIAN DOLLAR EXCHANGE RATES

$1	= $0.74 US	$1 US	= $1.35
$1	= 48 p	1£	= $2.10
$1	= $0.93 Aust	$1 Aust	= $1.07
$1	= $1.05NZ	$1 NZ	= $0.95
$1	= 0.86 SF	1 SF	= $1.16
$1	= 2.17 BF	1 BF	= $0.46
$1	= 1.06 DM	1 DM	= $0.94
$1	= 88 pesetas	100 pta	= $1.12
$1	= 1123 lira	1000 lira	= $0.89

Prices in this guide are in Canadian dollars.

orders are another means of having money sent from abroad. No commission is charged but it takes time. People who have residence status, permanent or not (such as landed-immigrants, students), can open a bank account. A passport and proof of residence status are required.

■ Currency

The monetary unit is the dollar ($), which is divided into cents (¢). One dollar = 100 cents.

Bills come in 2, 5, 10, 20, 50, 100, 500 and 1000 dollar denominations, and coins come in 1 (pennies), 5 (nickels), 10 (dimes), 25 (quarters) cent pieces, and in 1 (loonies) dollar and 2 dollar coins. The new 2 dollar coin will eventually replace the 2 dollar bill, though the bill will remain legal tender.

Climate and Clothing

■ Climate

The climate of Western Canada varies widely from one region to another. The Vancouver area benefits from a sort of micro-climate thanks to its geographic location between the Pacific Ocean and the mountains. Temperatures in Vancouver vary between 0°C and 15°C in the winter and much warmer in the summer.

If you plan on visiting other regions in Western Canada keep in mind factors like wind and altitude, which can cause a variety of weather conditions. Winters are cold and dry and temperatures can drop to -40°C, though the average is about -20°C. Summers are dry, with temperatures staying steady around 25°C in the south and lower in the mountains.

Winter

Vancouver has a particularly wet winter so don't forget your raincoat. In southern British Columbia the mercury rarely falls below 0°C. December to March remains the ideal season for winter-sports enthusiasts, who can enjoy many activities not far from the city (skiing, skating, etc.). Warm clothing is essential during this season (coat, scarf, hat, gloves, wool sweaters and boots) if you plan on visiting the mountains

Spring and Fall

In Vancouver, spring and fall, and winter too for that matter, are hardly discernable. Spring is short (end of March to end of May), and conditions are generally rainy. Warmer temperatures encourage a beautiful blossoming of flowers. Fall is often cool and wet. A sweater, scarf, gloves, windbreaker and of course an umbrella are recommended for these tow seasons.

Summer

Summer lasts from May to the end of August. Bring along t-shirts, lightweight shirts and pants, shorts and sunglasses; a sweater or light jacket is a good idea for evenings. If you plan on doing any hiking, remember that temperatures are cooler at higher altitudes.

Health

■ General Information

Vaccinations are not necessary for people coming from Europe, the United States, Australia and New Zealand. On the other hand, it is strongly suggested, particularly for medium or long-term stays, that visitors take out health and accident insurance. There are different types so it is best to shop around. Bring along all medication, especially prescription medicine. Unless otherwise stated, the water is drinkable throughout Western Canada.

During the summer, always protect yourself against sunburn. It is often hard to feel your skin getting burned by the sun on windy days. Do not forget to bring sun screen!

Canadians from outside British Columbia should take note that in general your province's health care system will only reimburse you for the cost of any hospital fees or procedures at the going rate in your province. For this reason, it is a good idea to get extra private insurance. In case of accident or illness make sure to keep your receipts in order to be reimbursed by your province's health care system.

■ Emergencies

The ☎ 911 emergency number is used in Vancouver.

 Shopping

■ What to Buy

Salmon: you'll find this fish on sale, fresh from the sea, throughout the coastal areas of British Columbia.

Local crafts: paintings, sculptures, woodworking items, ceramics, copper-based enamels, weaving, etc.

Native Arts & Crafts: beautiful native sculptures made from different types of stone, wood and even animal bone are available, though they are generally quite expensive. Make sure the sculpture is authentic by asking for a certificate of authenticity issued by the Canadian government.

 Accommodations

A wide choice of types of accommodation to fit every budget is available in Vancouver. Most places are very comfortable and offer a number of extra services. Prices vary according to the type of accommodation and the quality-to-price ratio is generally good, but remember to add the 7% G.S.T (federal Goods and Services Tax) and the provincial sales tax of 7%. The Goods and Services Tax is refundable for non-residents in certain cases (see p 43). A credit card will make reserving a room much easier, since in many cases payment for the first night is required.

Many hotels offer corporate discounts as well as discounts for automobile club (CAA, AAA) members. Be sure to ask about these special rates as they are generally very easy to obtain. Furthermore, check in the travel brochures given out at tourist offices as there are often coupons inside.

■ **Hotels**

Hotels rooms abound, and range from modest to luxurious. Most hotel rooms come equipped with a private bathroom. There are several internationally reputed hotels in Vancouver.

■ **Inns**

Often set up in beautiful historic houses, inns offer quality lodging. There are a lot of these establishments which are more charming and usually more picturesque than hotels. Many are decorated with beautiful period furniture. Breakfast is often included.

■ Bed and Breakfasts

Unlike hotels or inns, rooms in private homes are not always equipped with a private bathroom. There are many bed and breakfasts in Vancouver. Besides the obvious price advantage, is the unique family atmosphere. Credit cards are not always accepted in bed and breakfasts.

■ Motels

There are many motels on the main access roads into the city. Though they tend to be cheaper, they often lack atmosphere. These are particularly useful when pressed for time.

■ University Residences

Due to certain restrictions, this can be a complicated alternative. Residences are generally only available during the summer (mid-May to mid-August); reservations must be made several months in advance, usually by paying the first night with a credit card.

This type of accommodation, however, is less costly than the "traditional" alternatives, and making the effort to reserve early can be worthwhile. Visitors with valid student cards can expect to pay approximately $25 plus tax. Bedding is included in the price, and there is usually a cafeteria in the building (meals are not included in the price).

Taxes and Tipping

■ Taxes

The ticket price on items usually **does not include tax**. There are two taxes, the G.S.T. or federal Goods and Services Tax, of 7% and the P.S.T. or Provincial Sales Tax of 7%. They are cumulative and must be added to the price of most items and to restaurant and hotel bills.

There are some exceptions to this taxation system, such as books, which are only taxed with the G.S.T. and food (except for ready made meals), which is not taxed at all.

Tax Refunds for Non-Residents

Non-residents can obtain refunds for the G.S.T. paid on purchases. To obtain a refund, it is important to keep your receipts. Refunds are made at the border or by returning a special filled-out form.

For information, call:
☎ 1-800-991-3346

■ Tipping

In general, tipping applies to all table service: restaurants, bars and night-clubs (therefore no tipping in fast-food restaurants). Tips are also given in taxis and in hair salons.

The tip is usually about 15 % of the bill before taxes, but varies of course depending on the quality of service.

Restaurants and Bars

■ Restaurants

Excellent restaurants are easy to find in Vancouver. The local specialty is without a doubt Pacific salmon. Every city has a wide range of choices for all budgets, from fast food to fine dining.

■ Bars and Discos

In most cases there is no cover charge, aside from the occasional mandatory coat-check. However, expect to pay a few dollars to get into discos on weekends. The legal drinking age is 19; if you're close to that age, expect to be asked for proof.

Wine, Beer and Alcohol

The legal drinking age is 19. Beer, wine and alcohol can only be purchased in liquor stores run by the provincial governments.

Advice for Smokers

As in the United States, cigarette smoking is considered taboo, and it is being prohibited in more and more public places. A by-law was recently passed in Vancouver that prohibits smoking in all public places where minors have access. This includes all restaurants and food courts in shopping malls, it does not include adult-only establishments which can designate smoking areas. The by-law applies only to the city of Vancouver proper, and therefore has limited scope, nevertheless check before lighting up!

Most public places (restaurants, cafés) have smoking and non-smoking sections. Cigarettes are sold in bars, grocery stores, newspaper and magazine shops.

Safety

By taking the normal precautions, there is no need to worry about your personal security. If trouble should arise, remember to dial the emergency telephone number ☎ 911.

Children

As in the rest of Canada, facilities exist in Vancouver that make travelling with children easy, whether it be for getting around or when enjoying the sights. Generally children under five travel for free, and those under 12 are eligible for fare reductions. The same applies for various leisure activities and shows. Find out before you purchase tickets. High chairs and children's menus are available in most restaurants, while a few of the larger stores provide a babysitting service while parents shop.

Weights and Measures

Although the metric system has been in use in Canada for several years, some people continue to use the Imperial system in casual conversation. Here a some equivalents.

1 pound (lb) = 454 grams
1 kilogram (kg) = 2.2 pounds (lbs)
1 foot (ft) = 30 centimetres (cm)
1 centimetre (cm) = 0.4 inch
1 metre (m) = 40 inches
1 inch = 2.5 centimetres (cm)
1 mile = 1.6 kilometres (km)
1 kilometres (km) = 0.63 miles

General Information

Electricity: Voltage is 110 volts throughout Canada, the same as in the United States. Electricity plugs have two parallel, flat pins, and adaptors are available here.

Illegal Drugs: are against the law and not tolerated (even "soft" drugs). Anyone caught with drugs in their possession risks severe consequences.

Laundromats: are found almost everywhere in urban areas. In most cases, detergent is sold on site. Although change machines are sometimes provided, it is best to bring plenty of quarters (25¢) with you.

Movie Theatres: There are no ushers and therefore no tips. Movie listings can be found in major newspapers. Movietickets are considerably cheaper on Tuesdays.

Museums: Most museums charge admission. Reduced prices are available for people over 60, for children, and for students. Call the museum for further details.

Newspapers: The two principal newspapers in Vancouver are the *Vancouver Sun* and the *Vancouver Province*.

Pharmacies: In addition to the smaller drug stores, there are large pharmacy chains which sell everything from chocolate to laundry detergent, as well as the more traditional items such as cough drops and headache medications.

Religion: Almost all religions are represented.

Restrooms: Public restrooms can be found in most shopping centres. If you cannot find one, it usually is not a problem to use one in a bar or restaurant.

EXPLORING

The following nine tours, each covering a different part of Vancouver, will help you fully enjoy the local sights. You can set out to explore the city's streets by taking Tour A: Gastown ★, Tour B: Chinatown and East Vancouver ★★, Tour C: Downtown ★★, Tour D: The West End ★, Tour E: Stanley Park ★★★, Tour F: Burrard Inlet ★★★, Tour G: False Creek ★, Tour H: South Vancouver and Shaughnessy ★★ or Tour I: The Peninsula ★★★.

Carrall Street serves as the dividing line between east and west in the centre of town. It also marks the border between Gastown, to the west, and Chinatown, to the east.

 Tour A: Gastown ★

Just a few steps from downtown, Gastown is best discovered on foot. The area goes back to 1867, when John Deighton, known as Gassy Jack, opened a saloon for the employees of a neighbouring sawmill. Gastown was destroyed by fire in 1886. However, this catastrophe did not deter the city's pioneers, who rebuilt from the ashes and started anew in the development of their city, which was incorporated several months later.

In the late 19th century, Gastown's economic development was driven by rail transport and the gold rush. The neighbourhood then became an important commercial distribution centre, but was later abandoned in favour of areas farther west. After a long period of decline, restoration was begun in the mid-1960s and continues to this day. Gastown's streets are now lined with little hotels, trendy cafes, restaurants, art galleries and souvenir shops and make for a pleasant stroll.

Start off your tour at the corner of Water and West Cordova Streets, at the west edge of Gastown, which is accessible from the Waterfront station of the Skytrain.

The **Landing (1)** *(375 Water Street)*, with its brick and stone façade, was a commercial warehouse at the time of its construction in 1905; today it is a fine example of restoration. Since the late 1980s, it has housed offices, shops and restaurants.

Walk east along Water Street.

Like many other 19th-century North American buildings, **Hudson House (2)** *(321 Water Street)* has its back to the water and the natural setting. Erected in 1897 as a warehouse for the Hudson's Bay Company, it was renovated in 1977 in order to accentuate the pure lines of its red brick arches. The **Gastown Steam Clock (3)**, at the corner of Cambie Street, uses steam conducted through an underground network of pipes to whistle the hours. In clear weather, this spot affords a stunning view of the mountains north of the city.

Farther along Water Street, you will see the steep roofs of **Gaslight Square (4)** *(131 Water Street)*, a shopping centre laid out around a pretty inner court (Henriquez and Todd, 1975). Nearby are the offices of the **Architectural Institute of British Columbia (5)** ★ *(103 Water Street; schedule and programme, ☎ 683-8588)*, which offers guided tours of Vancouver during summertime.

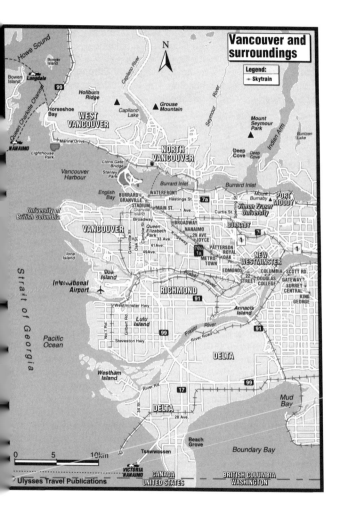

Vancouver and surroundings

Legend:
→ Skytrain

Ulysses Travel Publications

The intersection of Water and Carrall Streets is one of the liveliest parts of Gastown. Long **Byrnes Block (6)** *(2 Water Street)*, on the southwest corner, was one of the first buildings to be erected after the terrible fire of 1886. It was built on the site of Gassy Jack's saloon; a statue of the celebrated barkeep graces tiny **Maple Tree Square (7)**. The thick cornice on the brick building is typical of commercial buildings of the Victorian era. Rising in front is the former **Hotel Europe (8)** *(4 Powell Street)*, a triangular building erected in 1908 by a Canadian hotel-keeper of Italian descent.

Head south on Carrall Street, then turn right onto West Cordova.

Lonsdale Block (9) *(8-28 West Cordova Street)*, built in 1889, is one of the most remarkable buildings on this street, which is undergoing a beautiful renaissance with the recent opening of several shops and, even more importantly, a number of cafes serving all different kinds of coffee made with freshly roasted beans. The coffee trend, which started in the American city of Seattle, less than 200 km from Vancouver, has really taken off along the old-fashioned streets of this neighbourhood. Long popular with artists, Gastown is now considered a tourist area, and unfortunately has become a bit pricey in places.

Turn left on Abbott Street.

At the corner of Hastings Street stands the former **Woodwards department store (10)** *(101 West Hasting Street)*, founded in 1892 by Charles Woodward. It closed exactly 100 years later, following the death of the Woodward family patriarch, and was converted into 350 apartments during the summer of 1996. In the early 20th century, this part of Vancouver was the economic hub of the city. The shift of business to the west had a powerful impact on the area, both socially and economically. Today, part of Gastown is quite poor, and there are many vagrants here. Groups like the Downtown Eastside Residents Association defend the interests of those whose lives have been disrupted by the neighbourhood's recent overhaul, attempting to convince authorities to convert abandoned buildings into housing for the needy, so that people won't be forced to move to other parts of town.

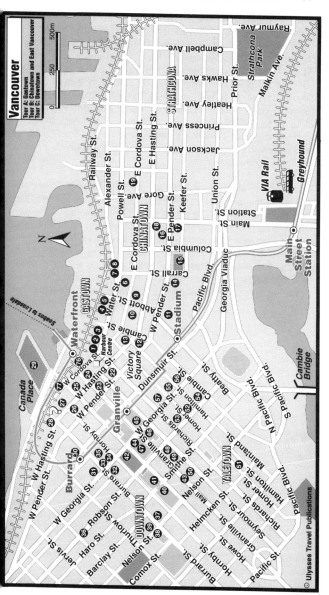

The south end of Abbott Street is dominated by the **Sun Tower (11)** ★ *(100 West Pender Street)*, erected in 1911 for the *Vancouver World* newspaper. It later housed the offices of the local daily, *The Vancouver Sun*, after which it was named. At the time of its construction, the Sun Tower was the tallest building in all of the British Empire, although it only had 17 floors. Caryatids support its thick cornice, while its polygonal tower is topped by a copper-clad Beaux-Arts dome. This part of town is developing at breakneck speed; the new buildings east of the Sun Tower are part of a big project known as International Village, which should attract hundreds of new residents to the area.

Turn right on West Pender Street to reach Cambie Street and **Victory Square (12)**, in the centre of which stands **The Cenotaph**, a memorial to those who lost their lives in the two World Wars. It was sculpted by Thornton Sharp in 1924. The square acts like a pivot between the streets of Gastown and those of the modern business district. Facing onto the north side is the elegant **Dominion Building (13)** ★ *(207 West Hastings Street)*, whose mansard roof is reminiscent of those found on Second Empire buildings along the boulevards of Paris.

Head north on Cambie Street to get back to where you started.

Turn left on West Cordova, where you'll find several triangular buildings, shaped in accordance with the streets, which intersect at different angles. Other buildings, with their series of oriel windows, are reminiscnet of San Francisco.

 Tour B: Chinatown and East Vancouver ★★

This tour starts at the intersection of Carall and East Pender. On East Pender Street, the scene changes radically. The colour and atmosphere of public markets, plus a strong Chinese presence, bring this street to life. The 1858 Gold Rush drew Chinese from San Francisco and Hong Kong; in 1878, railway construction brought thousands more Chinese to British Columbia. This community resisted many hard blows that might have ended its presence in the province. At the beginning of the 20th century, the Canadian government imposed a heavy tax on new Chinese immigrants, and then banned Chinese immigration altogether from 1923 to 1947. Today, the local Chinese community is growing rapidly due to the massive influx of immigrants from Hong Kong, and Vancouver's Chinatown has become one of the largest in all of North America.

On your way into Chinatown, you'll see the strange little **Sam Kee Building (14)** *(8 West Pender Street)*, which occupies a leftover piece of land barely 2 m deep. Its interior space is augmented by the oriel windows overhanging the sidewalk and a basement that extends under the street. This area was once home to several famous brothels, as well as a number of opium dens.

Take East Pender Street into the heart of Chinatown.

It is well worth stopping in at the **Sun Yat-Sen Garden ★ (15)** *($4.50; Oct to Apr, every day 10am to 4:30pm; May to Sep, every day 10am to 8pm; 578 Carrall Street, ☎ 689-7133)*, behind the traditional portal of the **Chinese cultural centre** at 50 East Pender Street. Built in 1986 by Chinese artists from Suzhou, this garden is the only example outside Asia of landscape architecture from the Ming dynasty (1368-1644). The 1.2-ha green space is surrounded by high walls which create a virtual oasis of peace in the middle of bustling Chinatown. At the beginning of the 20th century, the Canadian government imposed a tax on Chinese immigrants, then banned Chinese immigration altogether from 1923 to 1947. Today, the local Chinese community is growing rapidly, due to the massive influx of immigrants from Hong Kong, and Vancouver's Chinatown has become one of the largest in all of North America. It is worth noting that Dr. Sun Yat-sen (1866-1925), considered the father of modern China, visited Vancouver in 1911 in order to raise money for his newly founded Kuomintang ("People's Party").

The architecture of the buildings along East Pender Street reflects the background of Vancouver's first Chinese immigrants, most of whom were Cantonese; take, for example, the deep, multi-story loggias on a number of the façades, such as that of the **Lee Building (16) ★** *(129 East Pender Street)*, built in 1907. To the left of this building is a passageway leading to a charming inner court surrounded by shops. During

Chinese festivals, the loggias along East Pender Street are packed with onlookers, heightening the lively atmosphere.

Turn left on Main Street.

At the corner of East Pender Street stands a branch of the **CIBC (Canadian Imperial Bank of Commerce) (17)** *(501 Main Street)*, whose architecture was inspired by the English baroque style. Faced with terra cotta, this colossal edifice was designed by architect Victor Hosburgh and erected in 1915. Another example of the English baroque revival style is the former **Carnegie Library (18)** *(at the corner of Main and East Hastings)*, now used as a community centre. This building owes its existence to American philanthropist Andrew Carnegie, who financed the construction of hundreds of neighbourhood libraries in the United States and Canada.

Turn right on East Cordova Street.

St. James Anglican Church (19) ★, which stands at the corner of Gore Street, is one of the most unusual buildings to be erected in Canada between the two World Wars. A tall, massive structure made of exposed reinforced concrete, it was designed by British architect Adrian Gilbert Scott in 1935.

Head south on Gore Street to admire all the exotic products displayed along East Pender Street or enjoy a meal in one of the many Chinese restaurants there. If you wish to leave no stone unturned in your exploration of Vancouver's ethnic neighbourhoods, take Gore all the way to Keefer, turn right, then take a left on Main Street to reach the Pacific Central Station (about a 5-minute walk). Take the Skytrain toward Surrey, and get off at the next station (Broadway). If you're driving, head east on Georgia Street, turn onto Prior Street at the viaduct, then take a right on Commercial Drive.

When you get off the Skytrain, head north up Commercial Drive.

The next part of town you'll pass through is known as **Little Italy (20)**, but is also home to Vancouverites of Portuguese, Spanish, Jamaican and South American descent. In the early 20th century, the Commercial Drive area became the city's first suburb, and middle-class residents built small, single-family homes with wooden siding here. The first Chinese and Slavic immigrants moved into the neighbourhood during World War I, and another wave of immigrants, chiefly Italian, arrived at the end of World War II. North Americans will feel pleasantly out of their element in the congenial atmosphere of Little Italy's Italian cafes and restaurants. A few of these are listed in the "Restaurants" section (see p 108).

Some of Vancouver's most spectacular attractions are located outside the downtown area. To conclude your tour of East Vancouver, head to the city of Burnaby to visit **Simon Fraser University (21)** ★★ (SFU), located about a half-hour from the centre of Vancouver. If you don't have a car, take Bus #135 to the campus. Otherwise, drive east on East Hastings Street, take a right on Sperling Avenue, then a left on Curtis Street, which turns into Gagliardi Way.

Perched atop Mount Burnaby, SFU looks like a huge spaceship that just arrived here from another galaxy. The campus offers a panoramic view of downtown Vancouver, Burrard Inlet and the towering mountains to the north — a breathtaking sight in clear weather. The main buildings of bare concrete forming the nucleus of the university were designed in 1963 by the Canadian West's star architect Arthur Erickson and his associate Geoffrey Massey. Their architecture reflects the influence of Japanese temples, European cloisters, Mayan ruins and the Californian practice of leaving large parts of the exterior open. The grouping is laid out around a large courtyard. There is also a mall, half of which is sheltered by a glass and metal structure, so that students can enjoy pleasant temperatures winter and summer alike, and find shelter from the region's frequent rainfalls.

 Tour C: Downtown ★★

On May 23, 1887, Canadian Pacific's first transcontinental train, which set out from Montreal, arrived at the Vancouver terminus. The railway company, which had been granted an area roughly corresponding to present-day downtown Vancouver, began to develop its property. To say that it played a major role in the development of the city's business district would be an understatement. Canadian Pacific truly built this part of town, laying the streets and erecting some of the area's most important buildings. Downtown Vancouver has been developing continually since the 1960s — a sign of the city's great economic vitality, which can be attributed to Asian capital and the English Canadian population's shift westward, toward the mild climes of the Pacific coast.

This tour starts at the corner of West Hastings and Richards. Head west on West Hastings, toward the Marine Building, which will be directly in your line of vision. This tour can easily be combined with Tour A, which covers Gastown and ends nearby.

Located opposite Harbour Centre, the former regional headquarters of the **Toronto Dominion Bank (22)** *(580 West Hastings Street)* exemplify the classical elegance of early 20th-century financial banking halls. The building has since been abandoned by the bank for one of the modern skyscrapers along Georgia Street. The former regional headquarters of the **Canadian Imperial Bank of Commerce (23)** *(640 West Hastings Street)*, a veritable temple of finance, met the same fate and now house shops. This building, with its massive Ionic columns, was erected in 1906 according to a design by Darling and Pearson, whose credits include the Sun Life Building in Montreal. Opposite stands the massive **Royal Bank (24)** ★ *(675 West Hastings Street)* building, designed by S. G. Davenport. The Italian Renaissance style banking hall is worth a look.

The **Sinclair Centre (25)** ★ *(701 West Hastings Street)* is a group of government offices. It occupies a former post office, and its annexes are connected to one another by covered passageways lined with shops. The main building, dating from 1909, is considered to be one of the finest examples of the neo-baroque style in Canada. A little farther, at the corner of Hornby Street, is an austere edifice built in 1913 by the **Crédit Foncier Franco-canadien (26)** *(850 West Hastings Street)*, a financial institution jointly founded by French and Quebecois bankers. On the other side of the street, the **Vancouver Club (27)** *(915 West Hasting Street)* is dwarfed by the skyscrapers on either side of it. Founded in 1914, it is a private club for businessmen, modelled after similar clubs in London.

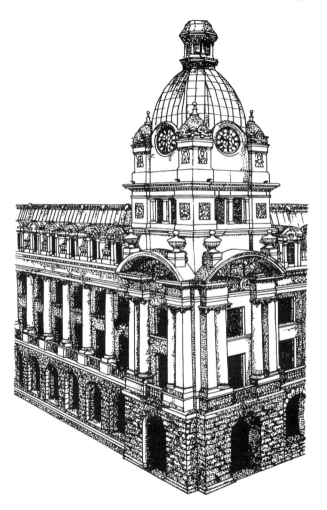

Sinclair Centre

The **Marine Building (28)** ★★ *(355 Burrard Street)*, which faces straight down West Hastings Street, is a fine example of the Art Deco style, characterized by vertical lines, staggered recesses, geometric ornamentation and the absence of a cornice at the top of the structure. Erected in 1929, the building lives up to its name, in part because it is lavishly decorated with nautical motifs, and also because its occupants are ship-owners and shipping companies. Its façade features terra cotta panels depicting the history of shipping and the discovery of the Pacific coast. The interior decor is even more inventive, however. The lights in the lobby are shaped like the prows of ships, and there is a stained glass window showing the sun setting over the ocean. The elevators will take you up to the mezzanine, which offers an interesting general view of the building.

Take Burrard Street toward the water to reach **Canada Place (29)** ★★ *(999 Canada Place)*, which occupies one of the piers along the harbour, and looks like a giant sailboat ready to set out across the waves. This multi-purpose complex, which served as the Canadian pavilion at Expo '86, is home to the city's Convention Centre, the harbour station where ocean liners dock, the luxurious Pan Pacific Hotel and an Imax theatre. Take a walk on the "deck" and drink in the magnificent panoramic view of Burrard Inlet, the port and the snow-capped mountains.

Take Burrard Street back into the centre of town and continue southward to West Georgia Street.

On your way, you'll see the giant **Bentall Centre (30)** *(at the corner of Pender Street)*, made up of three towers designed by architect Frank Musson and erected between 1965 and 1975. You'll also see the **Royal Centre (31)** *(1055 West Georgia Street)*, which includes the 38-story Royal Bank tower. These skyscrapers have to be "low" and squat in order to withstand the seismic activity in the Pacific Fire Crown.

The imposing **Hotel Vancouver (32)** ★ *(900 West Georgia Street)*, a veritable monument to the Canadian railway companies that built it between 1928 and 1939, stands at the corner of West Georgia Street. For many years, its high copper roof served as the principal symbol of Vancouver abroad. Like all major Canadian cities, Vancouver had to have a Château-style hotel. Make sure to take a look at the gargoyles near the top and the bas-reliefs at the entrance, which depict an ocean liner and a moving locomotive.

The 23-story building dwarfs the tiny **Christ Church Cathedral (33)** *(690 Burrard Street)* facing it. This Gothic Revival Anglican cathedral was built in 1889, back when Vancouver was no more than a large village. Its skeleton, made of Douglas fir, is visible from inside. What is most interesting about the cathedral, however, is neither its size nor its ornamentation, but simply the fact that it has survived in this part of town, which is continually being rebuilt.

Flanking the cathedral to the east are the shops and offices of **Cathedral Place (34)** *(925 West Georgia Street)*, built in 1991. Its pseudo-medieval gargoyles have not managed to make people forget about the Art Deco style Georgia Medical Building, which once occupied this site, and whose demolition in 1989 prompted a nation-wide outcry. Even with rock singer Bryan Adams's help, a major campaign to save the building proved futile. Cathedral Place is thus a building that is trying to gain acceptance; its pointed roof was modelled after that of the neighbouring hotel, and it is adorned with the stone nurses that once graced the Georgia Medical Building. The **Canadian Craft Museum (35)** *($4; Mon to Sat 9:30am to 5:30pm, Sun and holidays noon to 5pm; 639 Hornby Street, ☎ 687-8266)* lies behind in a pretty little garden integrated into the project. This small, recently built spot houses a sampling of Canadian handicrafts production and a few decorative elements that were part of the Georgia Medical Building.

Head west on West Georgia Street.

Turn left on Thurlow Street and left again on **Robson Street (36)** ★, which is lined with fashionable boutiques, elaborately decorated restaurants and West Coast-style cafes. People sit at the tables outside, enjoying the fine weather and watching the motley crowd strolling by nonchalantly. This activity has become a veritable mania among coffee lovers; an American celebrity passing through Vancouver marvelled at the number of cafes on Robson Street, going so far as to declare that Vancouverites were addicted to coffee, but that that hadn't changed the tempo of life here, which is known to be quite laid back. In the mid-20th century, a small German community settled around Robson Street, dubbing it Robsonstrasse, a nickname it bears to this day.

Return to Burrard Street, turn right and continue to Nelson Street.

The former **B.C. Hydro Building (37)** ★ *(970 Burrard Street)*, at the corner of Nelson and Burrard, was once the head office of the province's hydroelectric company. In 1993, it was converted into a 242-unit co-op and renamed The Electra. Designed in 1955 by local architects Thompson, Berwick and Pratt, it is considered to be one of the most sophisticated skyscrapers of that era in all of North America. The ground floor is adorned with a mural and a mosaic in shades of grey, blue and green, executed by artist B.C. Binning. On the other side of the street stands **St. Andrew's Wesley United Church (38)**, which was built in 1931 and houses a window created by master glassworker Gabriel Loire of Chartres, France in 1969. The **First Baptist Church (39)** *(969 Burrard Street)*, located opposite, was erected in 1911.

Walk east on Nelson Street.

Turn left on Howe Street to view the **Provincial Law Courts (40)** ★ *(800 Smithe Street)* (1978), designed by talented Vancouver architect Arthur Erickson. The vast interior space, accented in glass and steal, is worth a visit. The courthouse together with **Robson Square (41)** *(on the 800 block of Robson Street)* by the same architect, form a lovely ensemble. Vancouver's luxuriant vegetation (sprinkled with an abundant rainfall), unlike anything else in Canada, is put to maximum use here. Plants are draped along rough concrete walls and in between multiple little stepped ponds over which little water falls flow. Shops, restaurants and a skating rink welcome passers-by.

The **Vancouver Art Gallery (42)** ★ *($6; May 3 to Oct 9, Mon to Wed 10am to 6pm, Thu 10am to 9pm, Fri 10am to 6pm, Sat 10am to 5pm, Sun and holidays noon to 5pm, closed Mon and Tue during winter; 750 Hornby Street, ☎ 682-5621 or 682-4668)*, located north of Robson Square, occupies the former Provincial Law Courts. This big, Neo-Classical Revival style building was erected in 1908 according to a design by British architect Francis Mawson Rattenbury, whose other credits include the British Columbia Legislative Assembly and the Empress Hotel, both located in Victoria, on Vancouver Island. Later, Rattenbury returned to his native country and was assassinated by his wife's lover. The museum's collection includes a number of paintings by Emily Carr (1871-1945), a major Canadian painter whose primary subjects were the native peoples and landscapes of the West Coast.

Continue along Howe Street.

Turn right on West Georgia Street, then right again on the **Granville Street Mall (43)** ★, the street of cinemas, theatres, nightclubs and retail stores. Its busy sidewalks are hopping 24 hours a day. The black skyscrapers at the corner of West Georgia belong to the **Pacific Centre (44)** *(on either side of Georgia Street)*, designed by architects Cesar Pelli and Victor Gruen (1969). A stainless steel sculpture by Greg Norris adorns the public square. Beneath the towers lie the beginnings of an underground city modelled after Montreal's, with 130 shops and restaurants. Opposite stands the Hudson's Bay Company department store (1913), better known as **The Bay (45)**. The company was founded in London in 1670, in order to carry out fur-trading operations in North America. In 1827, it became one of the first enterprises to set up shop in British Columbia. Across the street stand the **Vancouver Centre (46)** *(650 West Georgia Street)*, which contains Scotia Bank's regional headquarters, and the **Vancouver Block** *(736 Granville Street)*, topped by an elegant clock. Finally, you can't miss the massive white **Eaton (47)** department store south of the Pacific Centre.

Stroll along the Granville Street mall heading south towards Theatre Row. You'll pass the **Commodore Theatre (48)** *(870 Granville Street, ☎ 681-7838)* and the **Orpheum Theatre (49)** ★ *(884 Granville Street, free tour upon reservation ☎ 665-3050)*. Behind the latter's narrow façade, barely 8 m wide, a long corridor opens onto a 2,800-seat Spanish-style Renaissance Revival theatre. Designed by Marcus Priteca, it was the largest and most luxurious movie theatre in Canada when it opened in 1927. After being meticulously restored in 1977, the Orpheum became the concert hall of the Vancouver Symphony Orchestra. Farther south, you'll see the vertical sign of the **Vogue Theatre (50)** *(924 Granville Street)*, erected in 1941. Today, popular musicals are presented in its Streamline Deco hall.

Turn left on Nelson and left again on Homer.

Located in the southeast of the downtown area, **Yaletown (51)** was an industrial area when the railways were still king. The growth of the trucking industry shifted business away from Yaletown's big warehouses, and the loading docks of Hamilton and Mainland streets have since been transformed into outdoor cafés and restaurants. A new group of tenants now occupies the old brick warehouses; designers, architects, film production companies and business people in general have brought this area back to life; trendy cafés and restaurants have followed suit.

At the corner of Robson Street is a curious building that is somewhat reminiscent of Rome's Coliseum. It is the **Vancouver Public Library (52)** ★★ *(free admission; year-round, Mon to Wed 10am to 9pm, Thu to Sat 10am to 6pm; Oct to Apr, Sun 1pm to 5pm, closed Sun in the summer; free guided tours Mon to Wed 12:30pm, 2pm and 7pm, Thu to Sat 12:30pm and 2pm; 350 West Georgia Street, ☎ 331-3600)*. This brand new building, is the work of Montréal architect Moshe Safdie, known for his Habitat '67 in Montreal and the National Art Gallery in Ottawa. The project stirred lively reactions both from local people and from architecture critics. It was chosen after finally being put to a referendum. The six-story atrium is positively grandiose. The **Ford Centre for the Performing Arts (53)**, completed in 1996, lies just opposite on Homer Street. Among other things, it contains an 1,800-seat theatre, whose orchestra seats, balcony and stage are depicted on the façade, north of the glass cone that serves as the entryway. These two buildings are sure evidence of Vancouver's thriving cultural scene.

Behind the library lies the long, low building of the **Canadian Broadcasting Corporation (54)**. The tubular structures on the façade are actually air ducts. The **General Post Office (55)** *(349 West Georgia Street)*, north of the library, was built in 1953. Hidden behind it to the east is the **Queen Elizabeth Theatre (56)** *(630 Hamilton Street)*, designed chiefly by Montreal architects Ray Affleck and Fred Lebensold. It contains three theatres of different sizes. Its opening in 1959 foreshadowed the construction of similar complexes across North America, including New York's celebrated Lincoln Centre and Montréal's Place des Arts.

Take Homer Street north, then turn right on Dunsmuir Street.

To conclude your tour of downtown Vancouver, stop by the city's Catholic cathedral, the **Cathedral of Our Lady of the Rosary (57)** *(at the corner of Dunsmuir and Richards)*, erected in 1899. The rusticated stone facing and the wood and metal clock towers are reminiscent of parish churches built around the same time in Quebec.

 Tour D: The West End ★

Excluding Vancouver Island, farther west, the West End is the end of the line, the final destination of that quest for a better life that thousands of city-dwellers from Eastern Canada have been embarking upon for generations. People come here for the climate and the vegetation, no doubt, but also to escape the hustle and bustle and constraints of the older cities in the central and eastern parts of the country. It should come as no surprise, therefore, that despite all its concrete skyscrapers, the West End has a laid-back atmosphere, influenced both by the immensity of the Pacific and the wisdom of the Orient.

Because of this westward movement, and the fact that there is nowhere to go beyond here, the West End has the highest population per square kilometre of any area in Canada. Fortunately, nature is never far, what with nearby Stanley Park (see p 67), the stunning views of the snow-capped mountains from the streets running north-south, or simply the sight of a cackling Canada goose strolling around a busy intersection.

This tour starts at the corner of Thurlow and Davie. Head west on the latter.

The population of the West End is a mixture of students and professionals, many of whom are getting rich, thanks to new technologies and the various new therapies now in fashion. The gay community is also well represented here. Residents of the local high-rises patronize the cafes, fast-food restaurants and grocery stores on Davie Street *(between Thurlow and Jervis)*. When you get to the corner of Nicola Street, take a look at the **Rogers House (58)** *(1531 Davie Street)*, christened Gabriola by its owner when it was built in 1900. It was designed by one of the most prolific architects of well-heeled Vancouver society, Samuel Maclure. The house, with its numerous chimneys and circular gazebo, originally belonged to sugar magnate Benjamin Tingley Rogers, a native of New York. At the turn of the 20th century, the West End seemed destined to become an affluent suburb with large houses surrounded by gardens. One street was even given the pretentious name of Blue Blood Alley. Things turned out otherwise, however, when the streetcar tracks were laid and a popular public beach on English Bay was opened in 1912. Gabriola is one of the only remaining houses of that era, and has since been converted into a restaurant.

Continue westward on Davie Street, then turn left on Bidwell Street to reach **Alexandra Park (59)** ★, which forms a point south of Burnaby Street. It boasts a pretty wooden bandstand (1914) for outdoor brass band concerts, as well as a marble fountain adorned with a brass plaque honouring Joe Fortes, who taught several generations of the city's children to swim. This luxuriant park also offers a splendid view of **English Bay Beach (60)** ★★ *(along the shore between Chilco and Bidwell Streets)*, whose fine sands are crowded during the summer. The apartment high-rises behind it give beach-goers the illusion that they are lounging about at a seaside resort like Acapulco, when they are actually just a short distance from the heart of Vancouver. Few cities can boast beaches so close to their downtown core. Fleets of sailboats skim across the magnificent bay, which has recently been cleaned of pollutants and is bordered to the west by the verdant expanse of Stanley Park (see p 67).

After dipping your big toe in the Pacific Ocean (it's that close!), head back into town on Morton Avenue, where you'll see the **Ocean Towers (61)** *(1835 Morton Avenue)*, a cluster of jazzily shaped apartment buildings dating from 1957 (Rix Reinecke, architect). The previous year, Vancouver had modified the zoning regulation for the West End so that these high-rises could be built, provoking a frenzy among real-estate developers and leading to the construction of an interesting group of buildings that is as 1950s and "piña colada" as Miami Art Deco is 1930s and "dry martini". The Ocean Towers' neighbour to the west, the **Sylvia Hotel (62)** (see p 101) *(1154 Gilford Street)* is the oldest building on the beach. Its construction in 1912 sounded the death knell of the West End's country atmosphere.

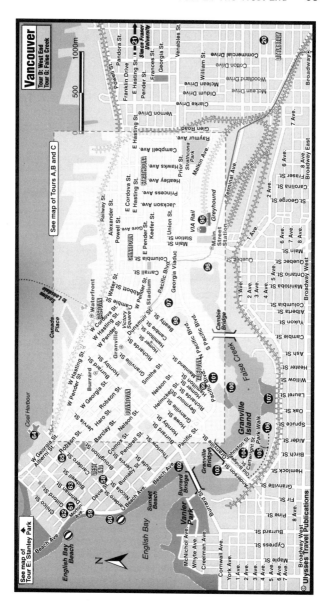

It is flanked by two post-modern buildings, the **Eugenia Tower** and the **Sylvia Tower**, topped in a very amusing fashion.

Head back east to Denman Street.

When they're not out surfing or sailboarding, the local beach bums often hang out around Denman and Davie Streets. The numerous restaurants in this area serve gargantuan brunches.

Continue north on Denman Street.

Denman Place (63) *(1733 Comox Street)*, at the corner of Comox Street, is a multi-functional complex made of bare concrete. Erected in 1968, it is home to the West End's largest shopping mall, complete with a supermarket, stores and movie theatres. The commercial area is topped by a 32-story tower containing apartments and a hotel.

Continue to the north end of Denman Street.

Take the path beside 1779 West Georgia Street to the waterfront and lovely **Coal Harbour (64)** ★, which offers some outstanding views of Stanley Park and the mountains. You will also be greeted by a rather strange sight along the docks: a kind of floating village made up of houseboats. The bay is full of yachts and sailboats, adding to the West End's seaside charm.

Go back to West Georgia, then take Bidwell south to Robson.

Head east on Robson Street, to the **Robson Public Market (65)** ★ *(at the corner of Robson and Cardero)*, a bustling indoor market with a long glass roof. You'll find everything here from live crabs and fresh pasta to local handicrafts. You can also eat here, as dishes from all over the world are served on the top floor. A pleasure for both the palate and the eyes!

If your legs aren't too tired, take Robson Street east, back to downtown Vancouver and Thurlow Street. On the way, you'll pass countless shops, some with very creative window displays. You can also head downtown on bus #19, which runs along Georgia Street (two blocks north). During the ride, you will be treated to some spectacular views of the mountains of North and West Vancouver.

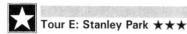

★ Tour E: Stanley Park ★★★

Lord Stanley, the same person for whom ice hockey's Stanley Cup was named, founded this park on a romantic impulse back in the 19th century, when he was Canada's Governor General (1888-1893). Stanley Park lies on an elevated peninsula stretching into the Georgia Strait, and encompasses 405 ha of flowering gardens, dense woodlands and lookouts offering views of the sea and the mountains. Obviously Vancouver's many skyscrapers have not prevented the city from maintaining close ties with the nearby wilderness. Some species are held in captivity, but many others roam free — sometimes even venturing into the West End.

A 10 km waterfront promenade known as the **Seawall** runs around the park, enabling pedestrians to drink in every bit of the stunning scenery here. The **Stanley Park Scenic Drive** is the equivalent of the Seawall for motorists. The best way to explore Stanley Park, however, is by bicycle. You can rent one at the corner of West Georgia and Chilco *(☎ 681-5581)*. Another way to discover some of the park's hidden treasures is to walk along one of the many footpaths crisscrossing the territory. There are numerous rest areas along the way.

From West Georgia Street, walk along Coal Harbour toward Brockton Point.

You'll be greeted by the sight of scores of gleaming yachts in the Vancouver marina, with the downtown skyline in the background. This is the most developed portion of the park, where you'll find the **Malkin Bowl (65)**, the **Brockton Oval (66)** and most importantly, the **Totem Poles (67)** ★, reminders that there was a sizeable native population on the peninsula barely 150 years ago. The **9 O'Clock Gun** goes off every day at 9pm on Brockton Point (it is best not to be too close when it does). This shot used to alert fishermen that it was time to come in.

Continue walking along Burrard Inlet.

On the left is the entrance to the renowned **Vancouver Public Aquarium and Zoo (68)** ★★★ *($9.50, children $6.25; Jul and Aug, every day 9:30am to 8pm; Sep to Jun, every day 10am to 5:30pm; ☎ 682-1118)*, which has the undeniable advantage of being located near the ocean. It displays representatives of the marine animal life of the West Coast and the Pacific as a whole, including magnificent killer whales, belugas, dolphins, seals and exotic fish. The zoo at the back is home to sea-lions and polar bears, among other creatures. The nearby **Miniature Railway (69)** is a real hit with kids.

Stanley Park harbours some lovely **flower gardens ★**, meticulously tended by a team of gardeners. Ask for Monsieur Gérard, a French gardener who has been working here for years; he'll show you "his" Stanley Park. Head back to the Seawall under **Lions Gate Bridge (70) ★★**, an elegant suspension bridge built in 1938. It spans the First Narrows, linking the affluent suburb of West Vancouver to the centre of town. The two enormous lion's heads that greet you as you head onto the bridge were carved by artist Charles Marega. There is talk of increasing the bridge's capacity, either by building an upper roadway or by erecting a twin bridge to the east. **Prospect Point (71) ★★★**, to the west, offers a general view of the bridge, whose steel pillars stand 135 m high.

The **Seawall Promenade** runs along the edge the park, and after rounding a 45-degree bend offers a panoramic view of the Georgia Strait, with Cypress Park and Bowen Island visible in the distance on clear days. Next, it passes **Third Beach (72) ★**, one of the most pleasant beaches in the region. The numerous cargo ships and ocean liners waiting to enter the port complement the setting.

We recommend stopping at the **Stanley Park Tearoom (74) ★**, located between Third Beach and **Second Beach (73) ★**. In the 1850s, the British government, fearing an American invasion (the U.S. border is less than 30 km from Vancouver), considered building artillery batteries on this site. The risk of such a conflict had diminished by the early 20th century, so a charming tearoom was erected here instead. The Swiss chalet-style building, surrounded by greenery, dates from 1911.

Complete the loop by taking the path to the **Lost Lagoon (75) ★**, which was once part of Coal Harbour, but was partially filled in during the construction of Lions Gate Bridge. It is now a bird sanctuary, where large numbers of barnacle geese, mallards and swans can be seen frolicking about.

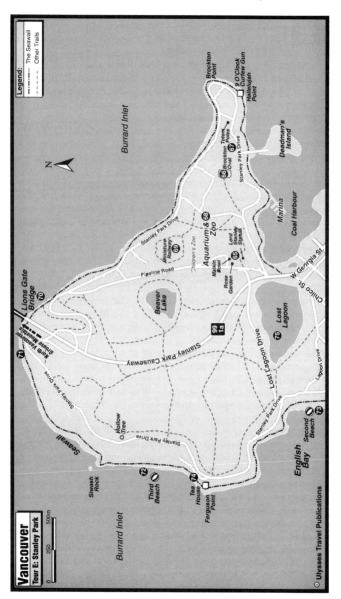

Vancouver
Tour E: Stanley Park

Legend:
- The Seawall
- Other Trails

0 250 500m

N

Burrard Inlet

Lions Gate Bridge

North Vancouver

West Vancouver

Siwash Rock

Seawall

Stanley Park Drive

Hollow Tree

Beaver Lake

Pipeline Road

Stanley Park Drive

Miniature Railway

Children's Zoo

Stanley Park Causeway

99 1a

Brockton Point

O'Clock Curfew Gun

Hallelujah Point

Totem Poles

Brockton Oval

Stanley Park Drive

Deadman's Island

Marina

Coal Harbour

Aquarium & Zoo

Lord Stanley Statue

Malkin Bowl

Rose Garden

Lost Lagoon

W. Georgia St.

Chilco St.

Lost Lagoon Drive

Stanley Park Drive

Lagoon Drive

Third Beach

Tea House

Ferguson Point

Second Beach

English Bay

Burrard Inlet

© Ulysses Travel Publications

Tour F: Burrard Inlet ★★★

Burrard Inlet is the long and very wide arm of the sea on which the Vancouver harbour — Canada's most important port for about twenty years now — is located. The Atlantic was once a favourite trading route, but the dramatic economic growth of the American West Coast (California, Oregon, Washington) and even more importantly, the Far East (Japan, Hong Kong, Taiwan, China, Singapore, Thailand, etc.), has crowned the Pacific lord and master of shipping.

Beyond the port lie the mountainside suburbs of North and West Vancouver, which offer some spectacular views of the city below. Along their steep, winding roads, visitors can admire some of the finest examples of modern residential architecture in North America. These luxurious houses, often constructed of posts and beams made of local wood, are usually surrounded by lofty British Columbian firs and a luxuriant blend of plants imported from Europe and Asia.

There are two ways to take this tour. The first is by foot, by hopping aboard the Seabus, which is the ferry that shuttles back and forth between downtown Vancouver and the north shore of Burrard Inlet, enabling passengers to enjoy the open air and take in some exceptional views of both the city and the mountains. The other option is to drive across Lions Gate Bridge (see p 68), take Marine Drive east to Third Street and head south on Lonsdale Avenue. The following descriptions refer to the walking tour, unless otherwise indicated.

Start off your tour in front of the Neo-Classical Revival façade of the former **Canadian Pacific station (76)** ★ *(601 West Cordova Street)*, which dates from 1912 and was designed by Montreal architects Barrott, Blackader and Webster. This station, Canadian Pacific's third in Vancouver, occupies a special place in the city's history, for before ships arriving from the west took over, trains arriving from the east fuelled the area's prosperous economy. In keeping with the times, the station no longer welcomes trains, but provides access to the Granville terminal of the Seabus. It also provides indirect access to the Waterfront terminal of the Skytrain (at the far end of Howe Street), but that's somewhat of a meagre consolation prize. Above the latter terminal is tiny **Portal Park** and its

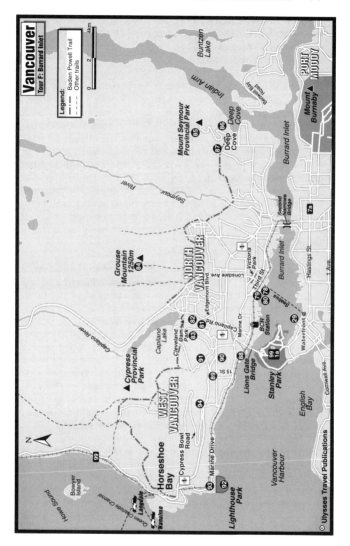

azaleas. **Granville Square (77)**, the skyscraper immediately to the west, is the only completed portion of a major real-estate development project (1971), which was to include the demolition of the train station.

Follow the signs for the Seabus. The crossing *($1.50)* takes barely a quarter of an hour, though you'll wish it were longer. The ferry lands at its northern terminal near the pleasant **Lonsdale Quay Market (78)** ★★, built on a quay stretching out into Burrard Inlet. The cafes surrounding the market offer an unimpeded view of Vancouver and the mountains, as well as all the activity at the nearby port, for the colourful tugboat dock flanks the market to the east. Built in 1986, Lonsdale Quay Market was the brainchild of architects Hotson and Bakker, who wanted to satisfy every basic human need here: food (ground floor), clothing (second floor) and lodging (upper floors, see p 104). From here, Vancouver really looks like a Manhattan in the making.

The market is the main urban attraction in North Vancouver, a suburb of 68,000 people sandwiched between Burrard Inlet and mountains over 1,500 m high. The urbanization of the north shore of the inlet began in the second half of the 19th century, when a number of businessmen from New Westminster decided to make capital of the firs, hemlock spruce and red cedars in the surrounding forest. It was Maine (U.S.A.) native Sewell Prescott Moody, however, who made British Columbia's wood known around the world. Ferry service between Gastown (see p 47) and "his" town, Moodyville, was introduced in 1866. At the beginning of the 20th century, most of the property in North and West Vancouver was transferred to British interests, who began developing the areas as residential suburbs.

North of the market, you can enjoy a pleasant stroll along Lonsdale Avenue. The old banks and public buildings bear witness to the prosperous past of the wood industry. Keep walking until you reach Victoria Park, then head west on Sixth Street to return to Burrard Inlet. On either side of the market, the east shore is scattered with tiny native reserves, some barely two blocks across. One of these is the **Mission Indian Reserve (79)**, centred around Mission Road, which leads to West Esplanade. There, you will find the **St. Paul Catholic Church (80)**, erected between 1884 and 1909 by Oblate missionaries from Quebec. The interior is decorated with stained-glass windows and polychrome statues.

If you are travelling by car, return to Marine Drive heading west and go up Capilano Park Road until you reach the **Capilano Suspension Bridge and Park (81)** *(adults $5.50, children $4; May to Oct 8:30am to 8pm; Nov to Apr 9am to 5pm; 3735 Capilano Road, ☎ 985-7474)*. If you are on foot at Lonsdale Quay Market, take bus number 236 to Edgmont Boulevard and ask the driver to show you where to catch the number 232. Paths lead to this metal cabled bridge, suspended 70 metres above the Capilano River, and which replaced the original bridge built in 1899 of rope and wood. The presence of Native Americans is more evident in British Columbian society than in any other Canadian province. A number of them gather in this park each summer to carve totem poles.

Three kilometres to the north is the **Capilano Fish Hatchery ★ (82)** *(free entry; 4500 Capilano Road, ☎ 666-1790)* the first pisciculture farm in British Columbia. This well laid out spot provides visitors with an introduction to the life cycle of the salmon. In the summer, Pacific salmon wear themselves out as they make their way up the Capilano River to reach the reproduction centre, making for an exceptional spectacle for visitors.

The upper part of Upper Capilano Road was renamed Nancy Greene Way after the Canadian skier who won the gold medal for the giant slalom at the 1968 Olympics in Grenoble, France. On the left, a road leads to **Cleveland Dam Park (83) ★★**, on the shores of Lake Capilano. The construction in 1954 of the impressive 100-m high dam at the centre of the park lead to the creation of the lake, Vancouver's main source of drinking water. Spectacular views of the neighbouring mountains, surround the park.

At the north end of Nancy Greene Way, there is a **cable car** *($14.95; summer Mon to Fri 9am to 10pm, Sat and Sun 8am to 10pm; ☎ 984-0661)* that carries passengers to the top of **Grouse Mountain (84) ★★★**, where, at an altitude of 1,250 m, skiers and hikers can contemplate the entire Vancouver area, as well as Washington State (in clear weather) to the south. The view is particularly beautiful at the end of the day. Wilderness trails lead out from the various viewing areas.

During summer, Grouse Mountain is also a popular spot for hang-gliding.

Among the other sights in North Vancouver that are accessible by car and worth mentioning, is **Mount Seymour Provincial Park (85)** ★★ *(Mount Seymour Parkway)* where both day and night skiing are possible. In addition, there are a number of cross-country trails, which become hiking paths in the summer. **Deep Cove (86)**, at the eastern edge of North Vancouver, on the shore of Indian Arm, is a fine spot for canoeing or kayaking. Close to the village is the head of the **Baden Powell Trail (87)** ★★, which runs through the wilderness all the way to Horseshoe Bay, 42 km to the west.

The Burrard Inlet walking tour ends at Grouse Mountain.

To return to Vancouver, get on the bus again, then take the Seabus back the other way. Motorists can continue exploring the area by heading to **West Vancouver** ★★ *(go back down Upper Capilano Road, then turn right on marine Drive)*, a fashionable residential suburb located on a mountainside. A number of talented architects have helped enrich the city's modern heritage.

Marine Drive leads past two large shopping centres. **Ambleside Park (88)** ★, located to the west of these, is worth a stop, as it offers some lovely views of Stanley Park and Lions Gate Bridge. Near the water, landscape architect Don Vaughan created the **Waterside Fountain** out of cubes of granite in 1989. West of the park, an attractive promenade leads along the water to 24th Street.

Turn right on 15th Street, then right again on Lawson Avenue, where you'll find **Pratt House (89)** *(1460 Lawson Avenue; not open to the public)*, designed by architect C.E. Pratt in 1948 for his own use. Pratt was a great promoter of this style of wooden house, which is open on the outside and blends into the natural environment. Although designed to withstand earthquakes and resist rotting, due to the heavy rainfall here (wide-edged roofs, cedar construction), these houses might appear fragile to Europeans more accustomed to stone and brick buildings.

The nearby **Berwick House (90)** *(1650 Mathers Avenue; not open to the public)*, designed by the architect of the same name, dates back to 1939, and was thus a forerunner of this type of construction. Since the 1930s, Canadian architects working on the West Coast have been greatly influenced both by the Californian buildings of the Greene brothers and Richard Neutra, and by much older Japanese designs dating from the time of the *shoguns*.

Head north on 15th Street, which becomes Cross Creek Road and then Eyremount Drive.

Next, you'll reach the **British Properties (91)** ★ *(on either side of the road starting at Highland Drive)*, where untouched woodlands and suburbia overlap. British Pacific Properties Limited, owned by London's famous Guinness family, known for their stout, began developing this mountainous area in 1932. The overall design was the work of the Olmsted Brothers, the worthy successors of Frederick Law Olmsted, whose credits include Montreal's Mount Royal Park and New York's Central Park.

Return to Marine Drive.

Turn right on Marine Drive and continue to **Lighthouse Park (92)** ★ *(entrance on Beacon Lane)*, located on a point that stretches out into the Strait of Georgia and has a lighthouse on its southern tip. Strolling around this peaceful place truly evokes a feeling of infinite space. The nearby **Gordon Smith House (93)** *(The Byway via Howe Sound Lane; not open to the public)* is a West Coast version of the glass houses of Mies van der Rohe and Philip Jonson. Designed by Erickson and Massey, it was built in 1965. Arthur Erickson, who is also mentioned in the previous tours, designed the Canadian embassy in Washington as well.

Like the TransCanada Highway, Marine Drive ends at the port of the village of **Horseshoe Bay** ★, where the terminal for the ferry to Vancouver Island is located. To return to Vancouver, head east on the TransCanada Highway, then follow the signs for Lions Gate Bridge. On the way, there is an exit for **Cypress Bowl Road**, a scenic road whose steep hills are ill-suited to cars with weak engines. It leads to **Cypress Park (94)** ★★★ and Cypress Bowl itself, a mountain where skiers can enjoy a

900 m vertical drop and breathtaking views of the Strait of Georgia.

Tour G: False Creek ★

False Creek is located south of downtown Vancouver and, like Burrard Inlet, stretches far inland. The presence of both water and a railroad induced a large number of sawmills to set up shop in this area in the early 20th century. These mills gradually filled a portion of False Creek, leaving only a narrow channel to provide them with water, which is necessary for sawing. Over the years, two thirds of False Creek, as explorer George Vancouver had known it in 1790, disappeared under asphalt. In 1974, when the local sawmills shut down en masse, people began moving into new housing developments the likes of which were becoming more and more popular around the world by that time. Then, in 1986, False Creek hosted Expo '86, attracting several million visitors here in the space of a few months.

Get off at the Skytrain's Main Street Station, located opposite the long Beaux-Arts façade of the **VIA Rail-Amtrak Station (95)** *(1150 Station Street)*. Determined not to be outdone, Canadian National (formerly the Canadian Northern Pacific Railway Company) copied Canadian Pacific by building a second transcontinental railway, which ran parallel to the first and ended at this station, erected in 1919 on the embankment of False Creek. Today, it welcomes Canadian VIA trains and American Amtrak trains, as well as various private trains which use the tracks running through the Rockies for scenic tours.

Head over to **Science World (96)** ★ *($9 or $12 with movie; 1455 Quebec Street, ☎ 443-7440)*, the big silver ball at the end of False Creek. Architect Bruno Freschi designed this 14-story building as a welcome centre for visitors to Expo '86. It was the only pavilion built to remain in place after the big event. The sphere representing the Earth has supplanted the tower as the quintessential symbol of these fairs since Expo '67 in Montreal. Vancouver's sphere contains an Omnimax theatre, which presents films on a giant, dome-shaped screen. The rest of the building is now occupied by a museum that explores the secrets of science from all different angles.

Science World

Walk alongside False Creek to Pacific Boulevard South before plunging into the void beneath Cambie Bridge.

During the summer of 1986, the vast stretch of unused land along the north shore of False Creek was occupied by dozens of showy pavilions with visitors crowding around them. Visible on the other side of an access road, **GM Place (97)** *(Pacific Boulevard South, ☎ 899-7400)* is a 20,000-seat amphitheatre, which was completed in 1995 and now hosts the home games of the local hockey and basketball teams, the Vancouver Canucks and Grizzlies respectively. Its big brother, the **BC Place Stadium (98)** *(777 Pacific Boulevard North, ☎ 669-2300, ≈ 661-3412)* stands to the south. Its 60,000 seats are highly coveted by fans of Canadian football, who come here to cheer on the B.C. Lions. Big trade fairs and rock concerts are also held in the stadium.

The new development on the grounds of Expo '86 is making good progress due to the city's thriving economy and the capital flowing out of Hong Kong on the eve of the British colony's return to communist China in 1997. There are plans to build high-rises containing thousands of apartments and flanked by gardens similar to those in the West End. The first phase of the project known as **Concord Pacific Place (99)**, named after a major Hong Kong real-estate developer, was completed in 1994. The high-rises, whose architecture resembles that of Battery Park City in New York, line Pacific Boulevard between Homer and Cambie Streets. A model of the entire project is on display at the **Concord Pacific Place Presentation Centre (100)**, on the waterfront.

The beautifully restored **CPR Roundhouse (101)** ★ *(at the corner of Davie Street and Pacific Boulevard)*, located opposite, is all that remains of the Canadian Pacific marshalling yard once located on this site. Erected in 1888, it was used for the servicing and repair of locomotives. The mammoth iron machines were pivoted around on single track so that they could be repaired behind one of the 10 doors of this "garage". Granville Island is visible across the water, as are the new residential areas along False Creek.

Follow Pacific Boulevard under Granville Bridge, then turn left on Hornby Street and right on Beach Avenue. This will lead you to the **Vancouver Aquatic Centre (102)**, a large indoor public pool and gym located on the other side of the Burrard Street Bridge.

The False Creek ferry docks are located behind this centre. Get on board the boat for **Granville Island and its public market** ★★ **(103)**. You'll notice the vaguely Art Deco pillars of the Burrard Street Bridge (1930). In 1977, this artificial island, created in 1914 and once used for industrial purposes, saw its warehouses and factories transformed into a major recreational and commercial centre. The area has since come to life thanks to a revitalization project. A public market, many shops and all sorts of restaurants, plus theatres and artists' studios, are all part of Granville Island. You will also find a community centre and the **Emily Carr College of Art and Design (104)**, which was enlarged considerably in 1996 and presents exhibitions of work by students and various artists from British Columbia. Not to be missed on the island is the micro-brewery tour offered by the **Granville Island Brewing Company (105)** *(Mon to Thu 9am to 7pm, Fri and Sat 9am to 9pm; guided tours every day at 1pm and 3pm; 1441 Cartwright Street,* ☎ *688-9927)*. Avoid taking your car onto the island; traffic jams are common, and parking is hard to find. To reach the island without following the False Creek tour take bus number 50 heading south from Howe Street downtown.

On the island, take Anderson Street south alongside Granville Bridge, then turn left on Park Walk.

You will now enter the **False Creek Development (106)** ★, a residential area begun in 1974 and built in stages by private developers on formerly insalubrious government land. It is pleasant to wander about on the pedestrian walkways around **False Creek Park (107)** and look at the carefully designed groups of houses.

Tour H: South Vancouver and Shaughnessy ★★

This tour covers two separate neighbourhoods located south of False Creek (see p 76), the City Hall area and the Shaughnessy Heights area.

In the 1930s, the municipal government planned to make the first area of this tour Vancouver's new downtown core, in an effort to shift the city centre. This involved building a new city hall near Broadway. It is true that when you look at a map, you realize that Vancouver's business section is located at the northern edge of town, on a peninsula accessible mainly by bridges. Practical as it was, however, the project was a bitter failure, as illustrated by the solitary tower of City Hall, rising up amidst scores of cottage-style houses.

The second area, Shaughnessy Heights, is an affluent residential enclave, which Canadian Pacific began building in 1907. It succeeded the West End as a refuge for well-heeled Vancouverites. The area was named after Thomas G. Shaughnessy, who was president of C.P. at the time and lived in the house of the same name in Montreal, which is now part of the Canadian Centre for Architecture. A number of local streets, furthermore, were named after the eminent families of Montreal's Golden Square Mile, like the Hosmers, the Oslers and the Anguses.

The tour starts at the corner of Cambie and Broadway.

Head south on Cambie Street to **City Hall (108)** *(453 West 12th Avenue)*, a massive, austere-looking tower topped by public clocks and featuring both classical and Art Deco elements (1935).

Head west on 12th Avenue.

Next, you will pass **Vancouver General Hospital (109)** *(715 West 12th Avenue)*, one of the largest hospitals in North America. Several of its buildings were erected in the Streamline Deco style between 1944 and 1950. Unlike the geometric, vertical Art Deco style, the Streamline Deco or "steamship" style features rounded, horizontal lines, which symbolize speed and modernism.

Turn left on Oak Street, then right on 16th Avenue.

Take Tecumseh Avenue into Shaughnessy Heights and walk around The Crescent to get a taste of the opulence of the houses in this area. Of all the houses, the most elegant is definitely the **Walter C. Nichol House (110)** ★ *(1402 The Crescent; not open to the public)*, a masterpiece by Maclure and Fox, built in 1912 for the former Lieutenant Governor of British Columbia. The half-timbering and mullioned windows typical of English farms and manors are clear reminders of the British roots that characterize this province, despite its great distance from the mother country. Furthermore, as the climate is similar to that of England, these houses boast front gardens as lovely as those found on the outskirts of London.

Steal along McRae Avenue, where you'll find the largest home in Shaughnessy Heights, **McRae House (111)** ★ *(1489 McRae Avenue)*, also known as Hycroft. Built in 1909 for General Alexander McRae, it was designed by Thomas Hooper. The long façade has a projecting portico in the Beaux-Arts spirit. The interior, decorated by Charles Marega, who sculpted the lions for Lions Gate Bridge, boldly combines Italian rococo with English neoclassicism. Like many other mansions across Canada, McRae House was abandoned by its owners and liveried servants after the stock market crash of 1929. Since 1961, it has been occupied by the University Women's Club.

Go back and complete the loop of The Crescent, then take Osler Avenue southward out of Shaughnessy Heights.

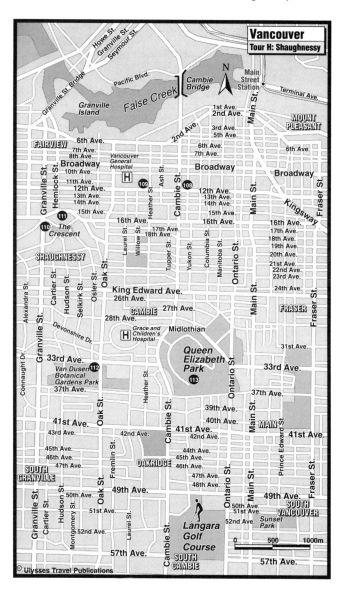

One of Shaughnessy's lovely residences

Turn left on 33rd Avenue, then right on Oak Street, where you'll find the entrance to the **Van Dusen Botanical Gardens (112)** ★★ *($2.50; summer, every day 10am to 9pm; winter, every day 10am to 4pm, closed Christmas; free tours Sun 2pm; 5251 Oak Street, ☎ 878-9274)*. Since Vancouver is so blessed by Mother Nature, a number of lovely gardens have been planted in the area, including this one, which boasts plant species from all over the world. When the rhododendrons are in bloom (late May), the garden deserves another star. At the far end is a housing co-op that blends in so perfectly with the greenery that it looks like a gigantic ornamental sculpture (McCarter, Nairne and Associates, 1976).

Farther east on 33rd Avenue is another magnificent green space, **Queen Elizabeth Park (113)** ★★ *(free admission; at the corner of 33rd Avenue and Cambie Street)*, laid out around the **Bloedel Floral Conservatory**. The latter, shaped like an overturned glass saucer, houses exotic plants and birds. The Bloedel company, which sponsored the conservatory, is the principal lumber company in British Columbia. This park's rhododendron bushes also merit a visit in springtime. Finally, the outdoor gardens offer a spectacular view of the city, English Bay and the surrounding mountains.

The walking tour ends here. Catch bus #15 on Cambie Street to go back downtown.

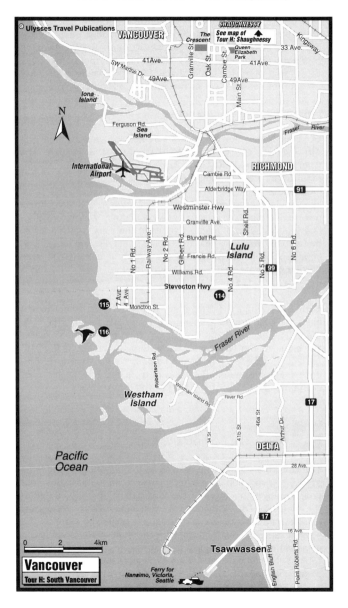

One of the other attractions in South Vancouver that visitors with cars can visit is the second biggest **Buddhist temple (114)** in North America *(every day 10am to 5pm; 9160 Steveston Highway, Richmond, ☎ 274-2822)*. To go there, take Oak Street southward toward Highway 99, which leads to the ferry for Victoria, and get off at the Steveston Highway West exit. Located between the third and fourth streets on your left, this place of worship has free entry.

Get back on the Steveston Highway heading west, turn left on 4th Avenue, and continue to the end of this avenue. The **Georgia Cannery ★ (115)** *(12138 4th Avenue, ☎ 664-9009)*, restored by Parks Canada, retraces the history of the fishing industry in Steveston. This historical spot explains the steps involved in conserving fish, especially salmon, and also shows how cod is transformed into pet food and oil. Very interesting. Leaving this establishment, stay along the seashore by way of the wooden walkway near the fishing boats. Fishing remains an important economic activity in this region. A commercial area with restaurants and shops invites you to relax. The day's catch is served in the restaurants.

Turn back along the Steveston Highway, this time heading east, and take Route 99 toward the ferry pier for Victoria; take the Ladner exit after the tunnel. Go along this road and follow the signs to the **George C. Reifel Bird Sanctuary ★★ (116)** *(adults $3.25; 5191 Robertson Road, Delta, ☎ 946-6980)*. Each year more than 350 species of birds visit this magical spot in the marshlands at the mouth of the Fraser River.

 Tour I: The Peninsula ★★★

The culture of the Pacific as well as the history and traditions of the native peoples are omnipresent throughout this tour which follows the shore of the vast peninsula that is home to the majority of Vancouver's residents. Posh residential neighbourhoods, numerous museums, a university campus and several sand and quartz beaches from which Vancouver Island is visible on a clear day all make up this tour. This is a driving tour as it extends over 15 km. The first four attractions are accessible aboard bus # 22 from downtown or by taking bus

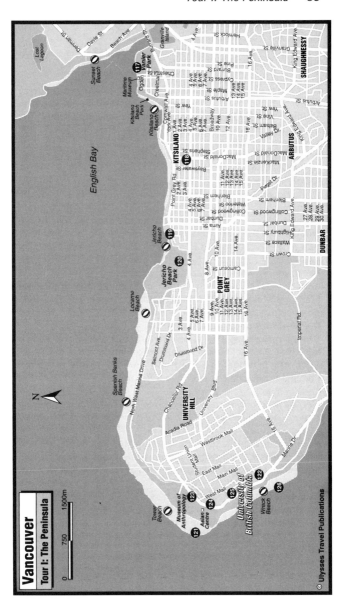

4 directly to the campus of the University of British Columbia.

Exit the downtown area by the Burrard Street Bridge.

Keep right, and immediately after going down the roadway leading off the bridge, take a right on Chestnut Street to get to **Vanier Park (117)**, which is home to three museums. The **Vancouver Museum ★★** *($5; every day 10am to 5pm; 1100 Chestnut Street, in Vanier Park, ☎ 736-4431)* forms its centrepiece. This museum, whose dome resembles the head-dress worn by Coast Salish Indians, presents exhibitions on the history of the different peoples who have inhabited the region. Of particular note is a lovely collection of native masks. At the entrance, an immense six-metre-high steel crab stands guard over the port of Vancouver, according to Indian legend. At the same spot is the **Pacific Space Centre** *($6.50; presentations Tue to Sun 2:30pm and 8pm, extra shows Sat and Sun 1pm and 4pm; ☎ 738-7827)*, formerly known as the H.R. MacMillan Planetarium, which relates the creation of our universe. It has a telescope through which you can admire the stars. The **Maritime Museum (17)** *($5; May to Oct, every day 10am to 5pm; Nov to Apr closed Mon; 1905 Ogden Avenue, ☎ 257-8300)* completes the trio of institutions in Vanier Park. Being a major seaport, it is only natural that Vancouver should have its own maritime museum. The key attraction is the *Saint-Roch*, the first boat to circle North America by navigating the Panamá Canal and the Northwest Passage.

Get back on Chestnut Street and turn right on Cornwall Avenue, which becomes a scenic road named Point Grey Road.

You will now pass through **Kitsilano** *(between Arbutus and Alma Streets)*, bordered to the north by a public beach. This area, whose wooden Queen-Anne and Western Bungalow Style houses are typical of the West Coast, was a middle-class neighbourhood in the early 20th century. If you want to leave no stone unturned during your tour of Kitsilano, take a left on MacDonald Street. Around number 2100, a lovely row of gabled houses, each with a veranda in front, forms a cohesive whole (1912).

Turn right on 6th Avenue, then right again on Bayswater Street.

Tatlow Court (118) *(1820 Bayswater Street)*, a group of neo-Tudor row houses built around a central court, is worth a quick look.

Turn left on Point Grey Road, then right on Alma Street, which leads to **Pioneer Park (119)**, home of the **Hasting Mills Store** *(1575 Alma Street)*. Built in 1865, this former general store is the oldest building in Vancouver. Originally located east of Gastown, near the city's first sawmill, it was transported here by boat in 1930 and then restored by the Native Daughters of British Columbia, a charitable organization, which, in spite of its name, has nothing to do with Native Americans.

Head south on Alma Street, then turn right on 4th Avenue.

Fourth Avenue runs alongside lovely **Jericho Beach Park (120)**, a green space and beach rolled into one at the edge of English Bay. Turn right on North West Marine Drive, then left on Belmont Avenue to see some of the loveliest houses on the peninsula. After, return to North West Marine Drive and head west to **Point Grey (121) ★★★**, also known as Pacific Spirit Park, which stretches out into the salt water, offering a full panoramic view of the Strait of Georgia.

The tour continues onto the grounds of the **University of British Columbia ★ (122)**, or UBC. The university was created by the provincial government in 1908, but it was not until 1925 that the campus opened its doors on the lovely site on Point Grey. An architectural contest had been organized for the site layout, but the First World War halted construction work, and it took a student demonstration denouncing government inaction in this matter to get the buildings completed. Only the library and the science building were executed according to the original plans. **Set Foot for UBC** *(May to Aug, free tours organized by students, ☎ 822-3777)*.

To this day, the UBC campus is constantly expanding, so don't be surprised by its somewhat heterogeneous appearance. There are a few gems however, including the **Museum of Anthropology ★★★ (123)** *($6, free admission Tue 5pm to 9pm; in the summer, every day 11am to 5pm, in the winter closed Mon and on Dec 25 and 26; 6393 North West Marine Drive; from downtown, take bus number 4 UBC or bus number 10 UBC; ☎ 822-3825)*, which is not to be missed both for the quality of native artwork displayed here, including totem poles, and for the architecture of Arthur Erickson. Big concrete beams and columns imitate the shapes of traditional native houses, beneath which have been erected immense totem poles gathered from former native villages along the coast and on the islands. Wooden sculptures and various works of art form part of the permanent exhibition.

On the edge of the West Mall is the **Asian Centre (124)** *(1871 West Mall)*, capped with a big pyramid-shaped metal roof, beneath which are the department of Asian studies and an exhibition centre. Behind the building are the magnificent **Nitobe Memorial Gardens ★★**, which symbolically face Japan, on the other side of the Pacific. Farther along, the **First Nations House of Learning (125) ★** is a community centre for native students, which was completed in 1993. It was designed to be a modern version of a Coast Salish Longhouse. The curved roof evokes the spirit of a bird (Larry Macfarland, architect). Totem poles surround the great hall, which can accommodate up to 400 people at a time.

The southwestern edge of the campus harbours a spot unlike anything else, **Wreck Beach ★** *(North West Marine Drive at University Street)*, where students come to enjoy some of life's pleasures. Nudists have made this their refuge, as have sculptors, who exhibit their talents on large pieces of driftwood. Vendors hawk all sorts of items next to improvised fast-food stands. A long stairway, that is quite steep in places, leads down to the beach.

OUTDOORS

Located where the mountains meet the sea, a short distance from the wilds of British Columbia, Vancouver offers an extremely wide range of outdoor activities. Downhill skiing, hiking in the woods, hang gliding, salt-water swimming in the Strait of Georgia, sun-bathing on sandy beaches, board-sailing and surfing can all be enjoyed just a half-hour or less from downtown.

The ski resorts of the Coast Mountains, north of Vancouver, are easily accessible by car via the Lions Gate Bridge. They boast substantial vertical drops (over 1000 m), and there is year-round cable car service to scenic lookouts on various mountaintops, from which visitors can take in outstanding views of the city. To the south, the beaches flanking the central neighbourhoods mean Vancouverites can go swimming in the ocean without leaving town — and the water isn't as polluted as you might think! Among the other popular activities, cycling and jogging in Stanley Park have become something of a ritual for many of the city's residents.

The local sports mania doesn't end there, however. Within the past few years, the city has built some impressive facilities for professional sports like football, hockey and most recently, basketball. This last sport, much more popular in the United

States than in Canada, is indicative of the growing influence of American culture here in Vancouver.

Beaches

The Vancouver shoreline is made up in large part of easily accessible sandy beaches. All these beaches lie along English Bay, where it is possible to walk, cycle, play volleyball and, of course, take a dip in the sea to fully enjoy the setting. Stanley Park is fringed by **Third Beach** and **Second Beach**, and then, farther east, along Beach Avenue, by **First Beach** where, on January 1, hundreds of bathers brave the icy water to celebrate the new year. A little farther east, **Sunset Beach** celebrates the day's end with gorgeous sunsets. At the southern edge of English Bay are **Kitsilano Beach**, **Jericho Beach**, **Locarno Beach**, **Spanish Banks Beach**, **Tower Beach** and, finally, **Wreck Beach** at the western edge of the University of British Columbia campus.

Kitsilano Beach is enlivened by beach volleyball tournaments and by an assortment of sports facilities, including a basketball court. Each year, contestants in a motorized bathtub race set out from Nanaimo on Vancouver Island, crossing the Strait of Georgia and ending at Kitsilano Beach. Locarno, Jericho and Spanish Banks beaches are quieter spots for family relaxation where walking and reading are key activities.

Hiking

Stanley Park is definitely the best place go hiking in Vancouver, with over 50 km of trails through the forest and greenery along the sea- and lakeshores, including the **Seawall**, an outstanding 8 km trail flanked by giant trees.

If you like gardens and are heading through Chinatown, you won't need a pair of hiking boots to visit the **Dr. Sun Yat-Sen Classical Chinese Garden** (☎ 689-7133), whose little bridges and trails will guide you through a realm of peace and serenity.

There are lots of places to go walking in the Point Grey area. Myriad trails crisscross the campus of the **University of British Columbia** (UBC). One of the best known runs across the famous **Endowment Lands**, which cover an area twice as large as Stanley Park. The others lead to the **UBC Gardens** (☎ 822-9666), administered by the university's botany department: the **Nitobe Japanese Garden** and the **Botanical, Alpine, Native, Physic, Food, Contemporary** and **Winter** gardens, which are all linked by well-marked paths. There is also a whole network of trails through the forest, and since UBC is located on a peninsula, all trails ultimately lead to the beach.

On the other side of Lions Gate Bridge, in North Vancouver, Capilano Road leads to **Capilano Canyon Park** (☎ 432-6350), where you'll find a trail offering sweeping views of the Capilano River. During summer, you'll be able to see the salmon swimming upriver.

Mountain hiking can be done on one of the peaks near the city centre. **Cypress Provincial Park** (☎ 926-5612), north of the municipality of West Vancouver, has several hiking trails, among them the Howe Sound Crest Trail, which leads to different mountains including The Lions and Mount Brunswick. The views over the west shore of Howe Sound are really quite spectacular. You must wear good shoes and bring good food for these hikes. To get to Cypress Park by the Lion's Gate Bridge, follow the signs west along the TransCanada Highway and take the Cypress Bowl Road exit. Take the time to stop at the lookout to contemplate Vancouver, the Strait of Georgia and, on a clear day, Mount Baker in the United States.

The hike up **Grouse Mountain ★★★** (☎ 984-0661) is not particularly difficult, but the incline is as steep as 25° in places, so you have to be in good shape. It will take about 2 hours to cover the 3-km trail, which starts at the cable car parking lot. The view of the city from the top of the mountain is fantastic. If you are too tired to hike back down, take the cable car for the modest sum of $3.

Mount Seymour Provincial Park (☎ 986-2261) is another good hiking locale, offering two different views of the region. To the east, is Indian Arm, a large arm of the sea extending into the valley.

A little farther east in this marvellous mountain range on the north shore, magnificent **Lynn Canyon Park** ★★★ *(☎ 987-5922)* is scored with forest trails. It is best known for its footbridge, which stretches across a gorge 80 m deep. Definitely not for the faint of heart! To get there, take Highway 1 from North Vancouver to the Lynn Valley Road exit and follow the signs, then turn right on Peters Road.

Lighthouse Park, in West Vancouver, is well suited to hiking on flatter terrain. From this site, you will be facing the University of British Columbia, the entrance to English Bay, and the Strait of Georgia. Take the Lion's Gate Bridge and follow Marine Drive West, crossing the city of West Vancouver and hugging the seashore until you reach the western edge of English Bay. Turn left at Beacon Lane toward Lighthouse Park.

If you get off the 99 just after the affluent suburb of West Vancouver and head west to Horseshoe Bay, you'll come to lovely little **Whytecliff Park**, located on the seashore. Most people come here to go picnicking or scuba diving. For an interesting little excursion, follow the rocky trail out to **Whyte Island** at low tide. Before heading out to this big rock, make sure to check what time the tides are due to come in, or you'll end up with wet feet.

A 15-min **ferry** *(BC Ferry, ☎ 277-0277)* ride from Horseshoe Bay, transports you to **Bowen Island** ★★★ *(☎ 947-2216)*, where hiking trails lead through a lush forest. Although you'll feel as if you're at the other end of the world, downtown Vancouver is only 5 km away as the crow flies.

 Cycling

The region has a multitude of trails for mountain biking. Just head to one of the mountains north of the city. A pleasant 8-km ride runs along the Seawall in Stanley Park. Bicycle rentals are available at **Stanley Park Rentals** *(676 Chilco Street, near Georgia Street, ☎ 681-5581)*. Outside Vancouver, you can go cycling in the Fraser Valley, near farms or along secondary roads.

Heading away from Stanley Park on the **Seawall** from English Bay, you'll reach another seawall, which is less crowded and better for cycling. About 15 km long, it skirts **False Creek**, passes in front of the recently built housing complex on the grounds of the 1986 World Fair, invites cyclists to stop in at Science World, leads to the markets on Granville Island and finally ends up back at the starting point on English Bay via the Burrard Bridge. More courageous visitors can follow the **Spanish Banks** beach all the way to UBC. You have to ride along roads during certain parts of the trip. To avoid getting lost, follow the green and white signs specifically aimed at cyclists.

The 15-min ferry ride from Horseshoe Bay out to little **Bowen Island** ★★★ *(☎ 947-2216)* is a worthwhile excursion. This perfectly lovely residential island has a network of quiet little country roads. You are likely to come across a deer or two, and make sure to keep an eye out for the eagles soaring overhead. After a day of pedalling, you can enjoy a relaxing drink by the harbour at Snug Cove.

Bird-watching

Birders should make a trip to the **George C. Reifel Bird Sanctuary** ★★ *(5191 Robertson Road, Delta, ☎ 946-6980)* on Westham and Reifel islands (see p 84). Dozens of species of migratory and non-migratory birds draw bird-watching enthusiasts year-round to see aquatic birds, birds of prey, and much more. Farther south, several species can also be observed at Boundary Bay and Mud Bay, as well as on Iona Island closer to Vancouver, next to the airport.

If you get off the 99 just after the affluent suburb of West Vancouver and head west to Horseshoe Bay, you'll come to lovely little **Whytecliff Park**, located on the seashore. Keep your ears tuned and your eyes peeled and you will probably spot some bald eagles in the tops of the tallest trees.

The largest bald eagle population in the world is found just 60 km from Vancouver, in **Brackendale**, which lies alongside the 99 on the way to Whistler. Winter is a particularly good time to visit. Eagle buffs mingle at the **Brackendale Art Gallery** *(P.O. Box 100, Brackendale, V0N 1T0,* ☎ *898-3333)*.

Windsurfing

The pleasures afforded by the sea in Vancouver are definitely not to be taken lightly. **Howe Sound,** located alongside Highway 99 North on the way to Squamish, was slated to become a major harbour for giant freighters, but to the great relief of local windsurfers never did. The wind rushes into the hollow formed by the mountains on either side of the fjord, making this part of British Columbia a paradise for high-speed board-sailing. You can obtain all the necessary information about where to go at the **Squamish tourist office** *(37950 Cleveland Avenue,* ☎ *892-9244)*. To find out about wind conditions, call the **Windtalker Windline** *(*☎ *926-9463)*. A ten dollar fee covers insurance and potential rescue costs.

Sea Kayaking

Like the mountains, the water is a key part of life in Vancouver, and there is an almost unlimited number of ways to get out and enjoy the sea. One option is to tour the city by sea kayak. **False Creek** stretches all the way to Main Street and Science World, and you'll pass Granville Island along the way; by paddling around **Stanley Park**, you can reach Canada Place and the skyscrapers downtown. More courageous visitors can set out along **Indian Arm** ★★★ to Deep Cove, an expedition likely to include a few encounters with seals and eagles. Kayak rentals are available at **Ecomarine Ocean Kayak Centre** *(1668 Duranleau Street, Granville Island,* ☎ *689-7575)* on **Granville Island**.

Sailing

Going for a sail is the best way to visit some of the lovely spots in **Vancouver Harbour**. Jericho Beach, in the Kitsilano area, is an excellent starting point. You can rent your own sailing dinghy or Hobie Cat at the **Jericho Sailing Centre Association** *(1300 Discovery Street,* ☎ *731-5415)*, or climb aboard a larger sailboat for a cruise of several hours or several days. The **Cooper Boating Centre** *(1620 Duranleau Street, Granville Island,* ☎ *687-4110)* is a good place to keep in mind.

 Pleasure Boating

Renting an outboard **motor boat** is as easy as renting a car. No special permit is required for you to putter around at your leisure or speed across the water, as long as you stay near the shore. You'll find everything you need at **Granville Island Boat Rentals** *(16296 Duranleau Street, Granville Island,* ☎ *682-6287)*.

 Salmon Fishing

Yes, it is possible to go salmon fishing in Vancouver. To do so, you must obtain a permit and rent out the necessary equipment from a specialized outfitter. This sport is quite expensive, but you'll get your money's worth of thrills, and you are virtually guaranteed not to come back empty-handed. The **Westing Bayshore Yacht Charters** *(1601 West Georgia Street,* ☎ *691-6936)* has an impressive fleet of fishing yachts.

Kite Flying

With its 26 km of beaches, Vancouver is the perfect place to go fly a kite. The most renowned spot for this activity is **Vanier Park**, which borders the beaches on English Bay, behind the Vancouver Museum. To get there, take the Burrard Bridge out of the downtown area and follow Chestnut Street through the pretty neighbourhood of Kitsilano. If you need equipment, **Kite Horizon Aerosports** *(1807 Burrard Street,* ☎ *738-5867)* has an infinite array of kites, including some high-performance models.

In-line Skating

In-line skating, more commonly known as Rollerblading, is a standard summer activity in Vancouver. Although you'll see skaters all over, the most popular place to go is around Stanley Park, on the **Seawall**, a fantastic 8-km trail flanked by a century-old forest. Skate rentals are available at many places along the beach, including **West Coast Board & Blade** *(☎ 675-9755)* and **Outa-Lines Inlines** *(1231 Pacific Boulevard, ☎ 899-2257)*.

Golf

Golf is a sport that can be enjoyed year-round in Vancouver, which boasts an almost limitless choice of greens. One of the loveliest is the **University Golf Club** at UBC *(5185 University Boulevard, ☎ 224-1818)*.

The oldest public golf course, the **Peace Portal Golf Course** *(16900 4th Avenue, Surrey, ☎ 538-4818)*, founded in 1928 and open year-round, lies along Highway 99, near the U.S. border, in the suburb of Surrey.

In Richmond, another of the city's southern suburbs, the **Mayfair Lakes Golf and Country Club** *(5460 No. 7 Road, Richmond, ☎ 270-0505)* has a top-notch green surrounded by water.

No golf course boasts a more spectacular setting than **Furry Creek** *(P.O. Box 1000, Lions Bay, ☎ 922-9461)*, located just past the village of Lions Bay, on **Howe Sound**, which Highway 99 North runs alongside on its way to Squamish. Nestled away in a splendid landscape, this course is more than just pleasant; imagine the sea stretched out beside towering, snow-capped peaks. Amazing.

Pitch & Putt

Pitch & Putt is a simplified version of golf. Although the rules are quite similar, you don't necessarily have to be a practiced golfer to play. For about twelve dollars per person (equipment included), you can spend a pleasant day with your friends or family outside among the flowers and impeccable greenery. Vancouver has three Pitch & Putt courses, the best known being the one in **Stanley Park** *(2099 Beach Avenue, ☎ 681-8847)*. The other two are in **Queen Elizabeth Park** *(P.O. Box 24611, Station C, ☎ 681-9947)*, which stretches south of town, and **Rupert Park** *(3401 East 1st Avenue, ☎ 257-8364)*, to the east.

Cross-Country Skiing

Less than a half-hour from Vancouver, three ski resorts welcome snow-lovers from morning to evening. In Cypress Provincial Park *(☎ 926-5612)*, **Hollyburn Ridge ★** offers 25 km of mechanically maintained trails suitable for all categories of skiers. These trails are frequented day and evening by cross-country skiers. Off-trail skiers can also venture here, as well as at **Grouse Mountain** *(☎ 984-0661)* and **Mount Seymour Provincial Park** *(☎ 986-2261)*.

Downhill Skiing

Skiing buffs will want to spend at least one day at **Whistler**, the number-one ski resort in North America, renowned the world over and located just a two-hour drive north of Vancouver. The resort's twin mountains, **Blackcomb ★★★** and **Whistler ★★★**, offer a vast skiable area, a 1,600 m vertical drop and an extraordinary 12 m of snow coverage every winter. Thanks to the top-quality, quadruple chairlifts, skiers only have to wait a maximum of 15 min at the bottom of the slopes, even on crowded days. A lift ticket will cost you over $50, but good skiing comes at a price!

ACCOMMODATIONS

Vancouver is a big city with lodgings for all tastes and budgets. All accommodations shown here are well located, within walking distance of bus stops and, in most cases, in or near the downtown area. **Discover British Columbia** (☎ 1-800-663-6000) can make reservations for you.

Tour B: Chinatown and East Vancouver

Simon Fraser University (*$30; sb, ℂ, ℝ, parking, no pets; Room 212, McTaggart-Cowan Hall, Burnaby, ☎ 291-4201, ≈291-5903*). This student residence is available from April to October and is located atop a mountain. If you bring a sleeping bag, a room for two costs about $30, saving you about $10. SFU is 20 km east of downtown Vancouver.

Tour C: Downtown

YWCA (*$48-73; sb or pb, tv, ℂ, ≈, no pets; 733 Beatty Street, ☎ 662-8188 or 1-800-663-1424, ≈ 681-2550*). This establishment is not restricted to women, and families are welcome. The building is brand new and offers rooms accommodating one to five persons.

Canadian Pacific Waterfront Centre Hotel *($120-$295; tv, ≈, parking, ℜ; 900 Canada Place, ☎ 691-1991, ✉ 691-1999)* is a Canadian Pacific luxury hotel located just a few steps from Old Vancouver. It has 489 rooms.

Radisson Hotel *(145 $; ≈, ℝ, ℜ, ◉; 8181 Cambie Rd; ☎ 276-8181, ✉ 279-8381)* is located near the airport and offers a high level of comfort. Rooms have coffee-makers and refrigerators, as well as work desks. Decor in the guest rooms, meeting rooms and restaurants is modern and classic, providing a relaxing atmosphere. A physical fitness centre and pool are well appreciated by some, especially during the rainy season. Next to the hotel is a very impressive Chinese supermarket; the hotel is located in Richmond, a suburb with a high percentage of Chinese residents. Upstairs from the supermarket is a Buddhist temple where visitors are received gracefully and can have the various aspects of Buddhism explained to them.

Once a Delta hotel, the **Metropolitan Hotel** *($160-200; tv, ℜ, △, ≈, parking; 640 Howe St., ☎ 687-1122, ✉ 649-7267)* is located right downtown, just steps from the business district. These luxury accommodations also have a luxurious price tag. The hotel's restaurant, Diva, with a pleasant staff and a cosy ambience, is worth trying.

Pan Pacific Hotel Vancouver *($199-$310; tv, ≈, △, parking, ℜ; 300-999 Canada Place, ☎ 662-8111 or 1-800-663-1515, ✉ 685-8690)* is a very luxurious hotel located in Canada Place on the shore of Burrard Inlet facing North Vancouver, with a good view of port activities. During their visit to Vancouver in 1993, Russian President Boris Yeltsin and all his entourage stayed at this hotel. It has 506 rooms.

 Tour D: West End

The **Oceanside Hotel** *($50-70; ℝ, C; 1847 Pendrell St., ☎ 682-5641, ✉ 684-4010)* is a small affordable hotel in the West End, and just a hop, skip and a jump from the beach.

Rooms with kitchenettes are available for longer stays. There are only 23 rooms so be sure to reserve in advance.

The **Greenbrier Apartment Motor Hotel** *($50-70; ℜ; 1393 Robson St., ☎ 683-4558, ⚎ 669-3109)* is particularly popular with globetrotters. You'll meet world travellers who have decided to take a break in Vancouver. Ask about weekly and monthly rates.

The affordable **Tropicana Motor Inn** *($50-75; tv, ℜ, ≈; 1361 Robson St., ☎ 687-6631, ⚎ 687-5724)* rarely has the "no vacancy" sign up. A great location right in the action on the busy part of Robson probably has something to do with it. It is not a palace, but is perfect for younger travellers or those on a budget.

Buchan Hotel *($50-85, children under 12 free; no smoking, bicycle and ski racks, tv, sb or pb, no pets; 1906 Haro Street, ☎ 685-5354, ⚎ 685-5367)* is located in the West End residential area near Stanley Park beneath the trees. At the end of Haro Street, on Lagoon Drive, three municipal tennis courts are accessible to guests. Other tennis courts, a golf course and hiking trails can be found near this 61-room, three-story hotel.

The **Robsonstrasse City Motor Inn** *($55; tv; 1394 Robson St., ☎ 687-1674, ⚎ 685-7808)* is another affordable Robson Street option. The clientele is similar to that of the Tropicana (see above).

Sylvia Hotel *($55-100; pb, tv, ℜ, parking; 1154 Gilford Street, ☎ 681-9321, ⚎ 681-9321 reserved for management)*. Located just a few steps from English Bay, this charming old hotel, built in the early 1900s, offers unspoiled views and has 118 simple rooms. People come for the atmosphere, but also to eat or for a drink at the end of the day. For those on lower budgets, rooms without views are offered at lower rates. The manager of this ivy-covered hotel is a Frenchman who is fully and justifiably dedicated to his establishment.

The **Barclay Hotel** *($65-100 bkfst incl.; tv, ≈, ℜ; 1348 Robson St., ☎ 688-8850, ⚎ 688-2534)* is an older though spotless establishment with direct access to a pricey restaurant.

West End Guest House Bed & Breakfast *($84-190 bkfst incl.; pb, parking, no pets, ⊗, no smoking, no children under 12; 1362 Haro Street, ☎ 681-2889, ⇒ 688-8812).* This magnificent inn set in a turn-of-the-century Victorian house is well situated near a park and near Robson Street. Minimum stay is two days. Evan Penner will be your host. Do not hesitate: the West End Guest House has a good reputation. (Nearby, at 1415 Barclay Street, is Roedde House, built in Victorian-Edwardian style in 1893 and designed by none other than the architect Francis Rattenbury, who also created the Vancouver Art Gallery, the legislature building in Victoria, and the Empress Hotel.)

The comfortable and simple luxuriousness of the **Riviera Motor Inn** *($100; tv; 1431 Robson St., ☎ 685-1301, ⇒ 685-1335)* is nevertheless a bit expensive.

Listel O'Doul's Hotel *($100-150; tv, ℜ, ◌; 1300 Robson St., ☎ 684-8461, ⇒ 684-8326)* on Robson also houses a friendly, though slightly noisy, pub and a good restaurant. The service and comfort are indisputable.

The **Blue Horizon Hotel** *($100-150; tv, ℜ, ◌; 1225 Robson St., ☎ 688-1411, ⇒ 688-4461)* recently re-opened after extensive renovations. Each of the 214 rooms affords an exceptional view of the city. Reasonably-priced meals are served in the interior "granite" decor or out on the terrace facing Robson Street.

The **Landmark Hotel** *($100-150; tv, ℜ, ◌, ≈; 1400 Robson St., ☎ 687-0511, ⇒ 687-2801)* truly is a landmark with it 40 floors and its revolving resto-bar at the top. The view is fascinating and an experience! The whole city unfolds before you in 90 minutes as the restaurant revolves 360°. The best time is at sunset as the sky darkens and the city seems to glow.

Coast Plaza at Stanley Park *($119-210; ≈, ◌, tv, ℜ, ℂ, ℝ, parking; 1733 Comox Street, ☎ 688-7711 or 1-800-663-1144, ⇒ 688-0885).* If you are looking for a big, modern, American-style hotel close to the beach, this 267-room establishment is a good choice. The restaurant serves everything, and the food is decent.

The **Parkhill Hotel** *($160-200; tv, ℜ, ◌, ≈; 1160 Davie St., ☎ 685-1311, ⇒ 681-0208)* is right in the middle of Davie Street in Vancouver's gay village. The rooms are perfectly comfortable and the restaurant serves fine Japanese cuisine. Just steps from English Bay and Stanley Park.

Hotel Vancouver *($160-295; ≈, ⊛, △, ℜ, parking; 900 West Georgia Street, ☎ 684-3131 or 1-800-441-1414, ≈ 662-1929)* belongs to the Canadian Pacific Hotel chain and was built in the 1930s in the *château* style characteristic of Canadian railway hotels, of which the Château Frontenac in Québec City was a precursor. In 1939 it hosted George VI, the first British monarch to visit Canada. You will find tranquillity and luxury in the heart of downtown near Robson Street and Burrard Street. The hotel has 508 rooms.

Pacific Palisades Hotel *($175-250; tv, ≈, parking, ℜ, ℝ, ℂ, no pets, ☺; 1277 Robson Street, ☎ 688-0461, ≈ 688-4374)* is part of the Shangri-La hotel chain. Its two towers, totalling 233 rooms, offer superb views of the sea and the mountains. Rooms facing north on the upper floors provide especially fine mountain views. A big pool and a well-equipped gymnasium are available to guests. All services for tourists or business travellers are looked after with professionalism. The staff are friendly and efficient.

Sutton Place Hotel *($215-295; ≈, △, ℜ, no pets, ☺; 845 Burrard Street, ☎ 682-5511 or 1-800-543-4300, ≈ 682-5513)*, formerly the Méridien, offers 397 rooms and the full range of five-star services normally provided by the top hotel chains. The European decor has been maintained. If you are a chocolate lover, don't miss the chocolate buffet served on Friday.

 Tour F: Burrard Inlet

The **Globetrotter's Inn** *($50; tv; 170 West Esplanade, North Vancouver, ☎ 988-2082)*, in the heart of North Vancouver, near the Seabus and the shops of Marine Drive and the Quay Market, is very affordable.

The **Grouse Inn** *($65; tv; 1633 Capilano Rd., North Vancouver, ☎ 988-7101, ≈ 988-7102)* located close to the Grouse

Mountain cable car is great for those who like to be near the mountains.

The **Horseshoe Bay Motel** *($70; tv; 6588 Royal Avenue, West Vancouver,* ☎ *921-7454,* ≈ *921-7464)*, in the chic neighbourhood of West Vancouver, is advantageously located near the charming little town of Horseshoe Bay, and the dock for the ferry to Nanaimo on Vancouver Island.

The **Canyon Court Motel** *($70; tv; 1748 Capilano Rd., North Vancouver,* ☎ *and* ≈ *988-3181)* is located right next to the Capilano Suspension Bridge, the Lion's Gate Bridge and the TransCanada Highway. It is very comfortable and not too expensive.

The **Lonsdale Quay Hotel** *($120, tv, ℜ; 123 Carrie Cates Court. North Vancouver,* ☎ *986-6111,* ≈ *986-8782)* is a luxury hotel set magnificently near the shores of Burrard Inlet, above the huge covered Quay Market. The rooms enjoy extraordinary views of downtown Vancouver.

 Tour H: South Vancouver and Shaughnessy

The **Best Western Abercorn Inn** *($90; tv; 9260 Bridgeport Rd., Richmond,* ☎ *270-7576,* ≈ *270-0001)* is relatively affordable for its category. It is located close to the airport and many shopping malls. A good choice for travellers looking for something halfway between the airport and downtown.

The **Delta Pacific Resort and Conference Centre** *($110 bkfst incl.; tv, ≈, ℜ; 10251 Saint Edwards Drive, Richmond,* ☎ *278-9611,* ≈ *276-1121)* is a pleasant hotel set amidst the shopping centres of Richmond, a small town about 30 minutes from downtown and nicknamed Chinatown II because of its large Chinese community.

The exciting spectacle of planes and seaplanes landing is part of staying at the **Delta Vancouver Airport Hotel and Marina** *($110 bkfst incl.; tv, ≈, ℜ; 3500 Cessna Drive, Richmond,* ☎ *278-1241,* ≈ *276-1975)*. This hotel offers all the amenities you would expect in a hotel of the Delta chain. It is located on the edge of the airport, close to the Fraser River.

Tour I: The Peninsula

Vancouver International Hostel *($15-19; men's and women's dormitories, sb, tv, cafeteria from Mar to Oct; 151 Discovery St., ☎ 224-3208, ⇒ 224-4852)*. Located in Jericho Park, this youth hostel is open day and night; take UBC bus no. 4 from downtown to reach it. With Locarno and Jericho beaches nearby, this is a great spot for budget travellers.

UBC Housing and Conference Centre *($20-95; sb or pb, ℂ, ℝ, parking, no pets; 5961 Student Union Boulevard, ☎ 822-1010, ⇒ 822-1001)*. These campus apartments are available from May to August. Inexpensive and well located, near museums, beaches and hiking trails, this spot also provides tranquillity.

Penny Farthing Inn Bed & Breakfast *($65-155 bkfst incl.; sb or pb, no smoking; 2855 West 6th Avenue, Kitsilano district, ☎ 739-9002, ⇒ 739-9004)*. Lyn Hairstock receives you warmly in her home built in 1912. Wood and stained glass give the four rooms plenty of charm.

John House Bed & Breakfast *($70-$140 bkfst incl.; sb or pb, no pets, Nov-Feb by request only; 2278 West 34th Avenue, Kerrisdale district, ☎ 266-4175)* occupies a magnificent, fully renovated house from the 1920s, with an extra floor added. The owners, Sandy and Ron Johnson, carried out the work; they also acquired several of the antiques that form part of the decor.

RESTAURANTS

This chapter will help you discover all sorts of great little eateries as well as the finest tables in the city, where local specialties as well as international delicacies can be enjoyed.

 Tour A: Gastown

Water Street Café *($; closes at 9pm; 300 Water St., ☎ 689-2832)*. A handsome bistro with big windows facing Gastown. Tables are decorated with pretty lanterns, and service is friendly. The menu centres around pastas prepared in creative ways.

The Old Spaghetti Factory *($; closes about 11pm; 53 Water St., ☎ 684-1288)* is an affordable, quality family restaurant. The turn-of-the-century decor is fun and the service is quick.

Top of Vancouver *($$$; Sunday brunch for $21.50; every day 11:30am to 2:30pm and 5pm to 10pm, until 11pm Fri to Sat; 555 West Hastings St.)*. This restaurant, located atop the Observatory Deck, revolves once an hour, giving diners a city tour from high in the air while they eat. Classic West Coast cuisine is served here.

Tour B: Chinatown and East Vancouver

Joe's Cafe *($; 1150 Commercial Drive)*. This spot is frequented by a regular clientele of intellectuals, Sunday philosophers and feminists, among others. What brings them together, most of all, is Joe's coffee.

Waa Zuu Bee Cafe *($; 1622 Commercial Drive, ☎ 253-5299)* is great and inexpensive. The innovative cuisine combined with the "natural-techno-italo-bizarre" decor are full of surprises. The pasta dishes are always interesting.

Nick's Spaghetti House *($-$$; 631 Commercial Drive, ☎ 254-5633)*. Copious meals are served on red-and-white-checked tablecloths, amidst landscape paintings of Capri and Sorrento. People are friendly here and patrons enter the restaurant through the kitchen, a reassuring element.

Santos Tapas Restaurant *($$; 1191 Commercial Drive, ☎ 253-0444)*. Latins seem to have a gift for calming the atmosphere with the aromas of their spices and with their music. This is certainly the case here where groups of musicians perform at your table. This restaurant is frequented mostly by Vancouverites.

The **Sun Sui Wah Seafood Restaurant** *($$; 4810-4818 Main St., ☎ 872-8822)* is a Chinese seafood place, the likes of which you will rarely see. With lobster, crab, oysters, *coquilles Saint-Jacques*, they have everything you could hope for and more. A must-try.

The **Cannery Seafood Restaurant** *($$$; until 10:30pm; 2205 Commissioner St., ☎ 254-9606)* is one of the best places in town for seafood. It is located in East End in a renovated century-old warehouse. The view of the sea is fantastic.

Tour C: Downtown

A relaxing ambience and family-style fare are served up at **Dining Car** *($; until 2am; 579 Dunsmuir St., ☎ 681-1625)*, where the clientele runs the gamut from suits to artists.

The **Hard Rock Cafe** *($; until 1am; 686 West Hastings St., ☎ 687-ROCK)* is part of the famous worldwide chain of restaurants where paraphernalia from famous rock stars and Harley Davidson gadgets decorate the walls, and delicious burgers and nachos are served.

Benny's *($; open 24 hours a day; 2503 West Broadway, and on Hamilton St., ☎ 738-7151)*. Stunning decor in a Yaletown loft. The furniture seems like something straight out of an artist's imagination: wooden tables with a giant screw as the central leg, chairs formed of a metal leaf with antennas sprouting, agave-shaped lamps, immense wooden tables seating a young but varied clientele. Elaborate lighting brings out the characteristics of this old building, in particular, its enormous wooden columns. Unfortunately, service is slow. Salads, bagels and desserts are served here. Strangely, there is no alcohol, though the place seems like a bar. Your server will find you by shouting your name when your meal is ready.

India Gate *($; 616 Robson St., ☎ 684-4617)*. You can get a curry dish for as little as $5.95 at lunchtime. In the evening, this restaurant is rather deserted. The decor is not at all exotic.

Known for its modern, sober and audacious decor, **Ciao Mein** *($$; until 11pm; 595 Hornby St., ☎ 669-6346)* serves Italian and Chinese food. Each dish boasts an exceptional presentation, and the grain-fed chicken is particularly excellent.

The **Yaletown Brewing Co.** *($$; closed midnight; 1111 Mainland St., ☎ 681-2739)* is a veritable yuppie temple in the post-industrial neighbourhood of Yaletown, and a fun place to pass an evening. Try the pizza from the wood-burning stove.

Le Crocodile *($$$-$$$$; 909 Burrard St., entry by Smithe Street, ☎ 669-4298)*. This establishment is the beacon of French cuisine in Vancouver, as much for the quality of its food as for its service, its decor and its wine list. Lovers of great French cuisine will be spoiled by the choice of red meats and the delicacies from the sea. The salmon tartare is a must, you *are* on the Pacific coast after all!

 Tour D: West End

Flying Wedge Pizza Co. *($; 1175 Robson St., ☎ 681-1233; 1205 Davie St., West End, ☎ 689-2850; 3499 Cambie St., ☎ 874-8284; 1937 Cornwall, Kitsilano, ☎ 732-8840).* Pizza lovers, these are addresses to jot down if you're looking for pizza that doesn't remind you of something you ate last week. Try the classic Beauty and the Beef pizza, with marinated beef, onions, bean sprouts, red bell pepper and cheese: a true delight! You'll get a discount if you bring your own plate, showing that you're ecologically correct.

Ciao Espresso Bar *($; 1074 Denman St., ☎ 682-0112).* At a time when governments are talking of prohibiting smoking in restaurants, cafés and bars, this little West End establishment is a veritable smoking room where folks come for the strong, dark brew and a good smoke. Neighbourhood atmosphere.

Starbucks *($; 1099 Robson St., ☎ 685-1099).* A green logo proclaims the spot. Capuccino, espresso, big, small, medium, strong, weak, decaf, with milk, cold with chocolate or nutmeg: the choice is yours. Charming terrace. Several other branches of this Seattle-based chain are scattered around Vancouver and surrounding areas.

Bread Garden *($; open 24 hours a day; 821 Bute St.; 1040 Denman St.; 1800 West 1st Ave.; 2996 Granville St. at 14th Ave.).* Appealing cafeterias with warm decor where everything is excellent, from the coffee to the bread, without forgetting the cheesecake and the salads. These are pleasant spots where you can eat well.

Da Pasta Bar *($; 1232 Robson St., ☎ 688-1288).* This Italian restaurant, located in the most refined part of Robson Street, offer original items such as pasta with curry. Full lunches for $7.95. Pleasant decor.

Luxy Bistro *($; 1235 Davie St.,* ☎ *681-9976)*. The menu of this little black-walled restaurant offers a list of hamburgers garnished with all sorts of ingredients and pasta dishes prepared with just as much imagination. Good quality and reasonable prices. People come for the atmosphere more than anything, especially on weekend evenings.

The **Kitto Japanese House** *($; until 10:30pm; 833 Bute St.,* ☎ *662-3333)* is the local teriyaki specialist, with inexpensive, quality dishes. Service is quick and the staff are friendly.

True Confections *($; until 1am; 866 Denman St.,* ☎ *682-1292)* is a dessert place par excellence with huge slices of cake. Be sure to try the divine Belgian dark chocolate torte.

O-Tooz, The Energy Bar *($; 805 Thurlow St.,* ☎ *683-0292)* is a healthy fast-food joint: fresh fruit juices, vegetable juices, low-calory sandwiches...

Kamei Sushi *($-$$; 811 Thurlow St.,* ☎ *684-4823; 1414 West Broadway,* ☎ *732-0112)*. This chain of Japanese restaurants offers excellent dishes at reasonable prices. Service is efficient and pleasant. A fine Asian experience.

Sakae Japanese Restaurant *($-$$ for lunch; 745 Thurlow St.,* ☎ *669-0067)*. It is easy to walk right past this restaurant, situated in the basement of a commercial building, but the welcoming smiles and the quality of the food compensate for its location. The sushi and sashimi will literally melt in your mouth.

The **Cloud 9, Revolving Restaurant** *($$; until 10:30pm; 1400 Robson St.,* ☎ *687-0511)* is an experience. This resto-bar at the top of the 40-story Landmark hotel offers an exceptional view. It takes 90 minutes for the restaurant to turn 360°. Sunset is a particularly picturesque as the sky darkens and the city begins to glow. Try the lamb chops or the salmon.

Raku *($$; north of Robson, on Thurlow St.)* A wealthy young Japanese clientele meets here and fits right in. It has the atmosphere of a noisy bar, but it is an ideal spot to begin a promising evening. The sushi and grilled meats are recommended.

Gyoza King *($$; 1508 Robson Street, ☎ 669-8278)*. The items served here range from teriyaki dishes to sashimi and include the chef's specialties such as anchovies marinated in alcohol and mustard. Warm atmosphere.

The Italian restaurant **Romano's Macaroni Grill** *($$; until 10:30pm; 1523 Davie, ☎ 689-4334)* is located in an enormous mansion. Fine olive oil on each table is just part of the cosy atmosphere. Children (and adults too) can draw on the tables with crayons provided by the restaurant. Go on a Sunday for the all-you-can-eat pasta brunch.

The **Fish House in Stanley Park** *($$; until 10:30pm; 8901 Stanley Park Drive, ☎ 681-7275)* is located in a Victorian house right in the heart of the park and just a few steps from the Seawall. Fine seafood and fish dishes are served in an opulent and lovely decor.

The Latin-American and Mexican cuisine of **Mescallero** *($$; until 1am; 1215 Bidwell St., ☎ 669-2399)* is served in a pretty setting with a friendly ambience; things get really busy on Saturday evenings.

Succulent French cuisine is served at **L'Hermitage** *($$$-$$$$; until 10:30pm; 1025 Robson St., ☎ 689-3237)*. Henri Martin, the former chef to King Leopold of Belgium, divinely prepares a variety of meat and seafood dishes.

The **Teahouse Restaurant** *($$$; until 10:30pm, along the Seawall, ☎ 669-3281)* serves delicious food and affords stunning views of English Bay from Stanley Park. Call ahead for reservations and for precise directions as it can be tricky to find.

The **Raincity Grill** *($$$; until 10:30pm; 1193 Denman St., ☎ 685-7337)* specializes in grilled fish and meats in true West Coast tradition. A bit pricey.

 Tour F: Burrard Inlet

Bean Around the World *($; 1522 Marine Drive, West Vancouver, ☎ 925-9600)*. A crowd of rather laid-back people squeezes into this warm, wood-panelled spot. Excellent coffees and sweets are served at reasonable prices.

Imperial *($$; Mon to Fri 11am to 2:30pm and 5pm to 10pm, Sat and Sun and holidays 10:30am to 2:30pm and 5pm to 10pm; 355 Burrard St., ☎ 688-8191)*. Located in the Marine Building, an Art Deco architectural masterpiece (see p 58), this Chinese restaurant also has several Art Deco elements, but it is the big windows looking over Burrard Inlet that are especially fascinating. In this very elegant spot, boys in livery and discreet young ladies perform the *dim sum* ritual. Unlike elsewhere, there are no carts here: the various steamed dishes are brought on trays. You can also ask for a list, allowing you to choose your favourites among the 30 or so on offer. The quality of the food matches the excellent reputation this restaurant has acquired.

The **Cafe Norte** *($$; 3108 Edgemont Boulevard, North Vancouver, ☎ 255-1188)* serves up an impressive menu of tangy Mexican specialties like enchiladas and fajitas, not to mention a zinger of a Margarita.

The **Boathouse** *($$; until 10:30pm; 6995 Nelson Ave., Horseshoe Bay, ☎ 921-8188)* is a large glassed-in restaurant at the heart of the quaint community of Horseshoe Bay. Seafood is its specialty: oysters, halibut, salmon...

The **Salmon House on the Hill** *($$$; until 11pm; 2229 Folkstone Way, West Vancouver, ☎ 926-3212)* serves up what is undoubtedly the best barbecue grilled Salmon; it is simply delicious. Built on the mountainside, the restaurant affords extraordinary views of Vancouver and the Pacific.

 Tour G: False Creek

La Baguette et L'Échalotte *($; 1680 Johnson St., ☎ 684-1351)*. If you expect to be picnicking during your visit to Granville Island, here is where you will find French bread, pastries, croissants and take-out dishes. Arlène and Mario take good care of this little shop, located in the heart of busy Granville Island.

The **Bridges Bistro** *($; until 11:30pm; 1696 Durenleau St., Granville Island)* boasts one of the prettiest terraces in Vancouver, right by the water in the middle of Granville Island's pleasure-boat harbour. The food and setting are decidedly West Coast.

Meat-eaters converge on **The Keg** *($$; until 10:30pm; 1499 Anderson St., Granville Island, ☎ 685-4735)*. There are lots of steaks to choose from and prices are reasonable. The atmosphere is relaxed and the staff particularly friendly.

 Tour I: The Peninsula

The Naam *($; 2724 West Fourth Ave., ☎ 738-7151)* blends live music with vegetarian meals. This little restaurant has a warm atmosphere and friendly service. This spot is frequented by a young clientele.

Sophie's Cosmic Cafe *($; 2095 West Fourth Ave., ☎ 732-6810)*. This is a weekend meeting-spot for the Kitsilano crowd, who come to stuff themselves with bacon and eggs. 1950s decor, relaxed atmosphere.

Issekaku *($; until 10pm; 2059 West 4th Ave., ☎ 737-0242)* is a friendly and reasonable Japanese eatery where you can enjoy sushi and fresh and fragrant *sunomo* salads.

The Funky Armadillo Cafe *($; until midnight; 2741 West 4th Ave., ☎ 739-8131)*, with its modern, unpretentious yet quality food, is considered the cocktail specialist of Vancouver. Frequented by a socially-aware clientele.

Las Margaritas *($$; until 10:30pm; 1999 West 4th Ave., ☎ 734-7117)* serves healthy Mexican fare in a lively setting with lots of ambience. A great place to go with a group of friends.

Sonona on 4th *($$; 1688 West 4th Ave., ☎ 738-8777)* is like three restaurants in one: it serves West Coast, Asian and Australian cuisines. The atmosphere is very mellow and the desserts are delicious.

Fiasco *($$; until 1:30am; 2486 Bayswater St.,* ☎ *734-1325)* is a yuppie hangout on the West Side whose parking lot is filled with Harleys on a regular basis. The food is Italian with pastas, pizzas, and the mood is relaxed with jazz in the evenings.

Raku Kushiyaki Restaurant *($$; 4422 West 10th Ave.,* ☎ *222-8188)*. The young chefs of this little restaurant prepare local cuisine served with oriental aesthetic rules in mind; they will help you discover their art. Take a meal for two to appreciate the spirit of this *nouvelle cuisine*, which encourages the sharing of meals among guests. The portions may seem small, but you still come away satiated. Ingredients are chosen according to the seasons, for example wild mushrooms served accented with garlic, green bell peppers, butter, soya sauce and lime juice. This dish may seem simple, and it is, but the taste of the food is not masked by some mediocre sauce. The meats and fish are also treated with subtlety.

Star Anise *($$; brunch for $13.50 Sat and Sun; every day 11:30am to 2:30pm and 5:30pm to 11pm; 1485 West 12th Ave.,* ☎ *737-1485)* is a very pretty and stylish restaurant frequented by the beautiful people. Big paintings adorn the yellow walls, and lanterns illuminate the tables.

Alma Street Cafe *($$; 2505 Alma St.,* ☎ *222-2244)*. Lovers of jazz trios and of excellent desserts have no hesitation in coming here. Kitsilano's young professionals frequent this spot, which is a bit expensive.

Located in Kitsilano, **Malinee's Thai Food** *($$-$$$; 2153 West Fourth Ave.,* ☎ *737-0097)* presents this oriental cuisine with taste and subtlety. The coconut milk and cashew sauces hold some surprises.

ENTERTAINMENT

ARTS Hotline (☎ 684-ARTS) will inform you about all shows (dance, theatre, music, cinema and literature) in the city.

For information on jazz shows in Vancouver, call the **Jazz Hotline** (435 West Hastings St., ☎ 682-0706).

The Georgia Straight (1235 West Pender Street, ☎ 681-2000). This weekly paper is published every Thursday and distributed free at many spots in Vancouver. You will find all the necessary information on coming shows and cultural events. This paper is read religiously each week by many Vancouverites and has acquired a good reputation.

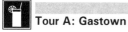
Tour A: Gastown

Town Pump Restaurant (66 Water Street, ☎ 683-6695). New alternative-music groups give shows at this Gastown stage. The place is very big, and you can play pool.

The Purple Onion Jazz Cabaret (15 Water St., ☎ 602-9442) has two floors with a D.J. on the first and an orchestra on the second. The music and the ambience are both terrific. The line-up on weekends can be ridiculous, however, so be warned.

The **Blarney Stone** *(216 Carrall St.)* is the spot for authentic Irish jigs and reels. The ambience is frenetic with people dancing everywhere, on the tables, on the chairs... A must-see!

Tour B: Chinatown and East Vancouver

If you're feeling lucky, try your hand at the **Royal Diamond Casino** *(750 Pacific Boulevard South, ☎ 685-2340)*. Casinos in British Columbia are government owned and all the winnings are donated to charity. A good system!

Tour C: Downtown

Commodore Ballroom *(870 Granville Street, ☎ 681-7838)*. This magnificent theatre has provided a stage for everyone, from pop singers to rockers. Take the time to try a few dance steps on the wooden floor resting on a cushion of tires. Weekend club nights attract a hopping crowd.

Royal Hotel *(1025 Granville Street, ☎ 685-5335)*. A gay crowd throngs to the 1950s decor here with a few '60s and '70s add-ons. Friday evenings are very popular, perhaps because of the live music, often country and western. People wait in line as early as 5:30pm, though Sunday evenings are more worth it.

Yale Hotel *(admission charged; 1300 Granville Street, ☎ 681-9253)*. Vancouver's blues temple. Each week, excellent groups appear before a varied crowd.

Railway Club *(admission charged; 579 Dunsmuir Street, ☎ 681-1625)*. Folk music or blues are presented in an oblong spot that brings to mind a railway car. A miniature electric train runs in a loop above the customers as they enjoy the musicians' performance.

Automotive *(1095 Homer Street, ☎ 682-0040)*. This interesting establishment recalls architectural influences from the 1950s, with a preponderance of stainless steel. A young clientele comes to the Automotive to play pool or to watch sports events on television.

The Odyssey *(1251 Howe Street, ☎ 689-5256)*. This big discotheque is very fashionable. It is much enjoyed by the gay community and is frequented by a young clientele.

The **CN IMAX Cinema** *(2nd floor, Canada Place, ☎ 682-IMAX)* consists of a seven-story-high screen and digital 2,000-watt sound. The IMAX system is an extraordinary audiovisual experience. Call for the schedule of 3-D films being presented.

The best night at the **Piccadilly Pub** *(620 West Pender St., ☎ 682-3221)* is Thursday, when groovy, funk and acid-jazz make up the line-up.

Bar None *(1222 Hamilton St., ☎ 689-7000)* is the hang-out of Vancouver's trendy youth. A friendly pub atmosphere is complemented with a dance floor. Watch out for long line-ups of Friday and Saturday evenings.

Richard's on Richard *(1036 Richard St., ☎ 687-6794)* is an institution in Vancouver. People of all ages flock to this chic spot to see and be seen. Theme nights. A must try.

For a heady night of techno music and dancing, check out **Lovafair** *(1275 Seymour St., ☎ 685-3288)*. Young crowd.

The **Yaletown Brewing Co.** *(1111 Mainland St., ☎ 681-2739)* is a popular yuppie hangout in Yaletown. The ideal spot for an evening with some friends and some brews.

The **Chameleon Urban Lounge** *(801 West Georgia Ave.)* boasts an elegant groovy and jazzy ambience. There is no cover during the week. Great music, but the drinks are a bit expensive.

 Tour D: West End

The Denman Station *(860 Denman Street, ☎ 669-3448)*. A neighbourhood bar that draws a gay clientele. Loud, popular music is played and videos are shown. Dancing late in the evening.

Celebrities *(1022 Davie Street,* ☎ *689-3180)*. This, the biggest discotheque in Vancouver, is visited by a mixed clientele.

Numbers *(1088 Davie Street,* ☎ *685-4077)*. This three-story bar, with rustic decor, is exclusively gay and has a clientele in the 25-to-40 age group. Pool tables, dancing.

The **Town Pump** *(66 Water St.,* ☎ *683-6695)* has live bands just about every night presenting everything from rock to jazz and reggae.

Roxy *(932 Granville at the corner of Nelson)* is a perennial favourite for its retro take on everything. Live bands and theme nights are often featured.

SHOPPING

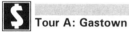

Y ou'll surely come upon all manner of interesting shops as you explore the city. To help you discover some of the best bets in Vancouver however, read on...

 Tour A: Gastown

Maxwell's Artists' Materials *(206 Cambie Street at Water Street)*. As its name indicates, this shop specializes in artists' materials.

The **Inuit Gallery of Vancouver** *(345 Water St., ☎ 688-7323)* sells some magnificent pieces of native art from Canada's far north and from the Queen Charlotte Islands.

 Tour B: Chinatown and East Vancouver

Rasta Wares *(1505 Commercial Drive, 255-3600)*. This shop offers incense and jewellery from India, Indonesia and Africa at low prices.

.iignlife Records & Music *(1317 Commercial Drive, 251-6964)*. This is the spot to find new wave and other types of music at good prices.

The **Ten Ren Tea and Ginseng Company** *(550 Main St.,* ☎ *684-1566)* is without a doubt the best tea shop in Canada. Big jars hold an exceptional variety of teas from around the world.

Tung Fong Hung *(536 Main St.,* ☎ *688-0883)* is a traditional Chinese herbalist. Ask for Liping, he will take the time to explain the complex healing powers of these plants. The shop specializes in ginseng.

Pacific Centre Mall *(underground at the corner of Howe St. and Georgia Ave.)* is a big shopping centre located right downtown. The latest in fashion from Paris to Tokyo, including of course the West Coast is available here. There are close to 200 shops.

Dorothy Grant *(757 West Hastings St.,* ☎ *681-0201)* makes clothing styled after that of the Haida Indians. The coats and capes are especially outstanding.

Odyssey Imports *(534 Seymour St.,* ☎ *669-6644)* specializes in imported music: funk, jazz, techno, on compact disc or vinyl. You can listen before you buy.

A&B Sound *(556 Seymour St.,* ☎ *687-5837)* has great prices in electronics, video cassettes and compact discs. Watch out for the crowds on weekends.

Value Vintage *(710 Robson St.,* ☎ *685-5403)* is an exceptional shop that both buys and sells vintage clothing from the glory days of rockabilly and disco.

Rocky Mountain Chocolate Factory *(1017 Robson St.,* ☎ *688-4100)* is a divine little chocolate shop. You can savour bulk chocolate with nuts and fruits, or perhaps the bitter, dark chocolate, for the real connoisseur.

Tour D: West End

Duthie's *(919 Robson St., ☎ 684-4496)* is *the* bookstore in Vancouver. With an exceptional selection of books and a friendly attentive staff, Duthie's has built itself quite a reputation. They recently opened a branch *(☎ 602-0610)* in the impressive new Vancouver Library (see p 62). The move has been a huge success leaving people wondering why no one thought of doing it before!

Douglas Coupland

Vancouver can be proud of its most recent star-author, Douglas Coupland, who in 1991 at the age of 30 published his first novel, *Generation X*. His work coined a new catch-phrase that is now used by everyone from sociologists to ad agencies to describe this young, educated and underemployed generation. Coupland's latest novel *Microserfs*, has proven just as sociological, but this time it is the world of young computer whizzes that he is describing, with sweeping generalizations about American popular culture that are both ironic and admiring; interestingly paralleling English-Canadian sentiment about the United States. Coupland works one day a week at Duthie's Bookstore *(4th Avenue)*.

Manhattan Books *(1089 Robson St., ☎ 681-9074)* sells major international magazine and newspapers as well as a respectable selection of books in French.

Little Sisters Book and Art Emporium *(every day 10am to 11pm; 1221 Thurlow Street, ☎ 669-1753 or 1-800-567-1662)*. This is the only gay bookshop in Western Canada. It offers gay literature as well as essays on homosexuality, feminism, etc. It is also a vast bazaar, with products that include humorous greeting cards. With the support of several Canadian literary figures, this bookshop has been fighting Canada Customs, which arbitrarily blocks the import of certain publications. Books by recognized and respected authors such as Marcel Proust have been seized by Canada Customs, which has taken on the role of censor. Some of the same titles bound for

Shopping

bookshops have mysteriously escaped seizure by Canada Customs, leading to questions about discrimination.

Stéphane de Raucourt Shoes *(1067 Robson Street, 682-2280)*. If you are looking for quality shoes that stand out from the ordinary, here is a spot to keep in mind. They are expensive, but a little window-shopping never hurt anyone.

Below the Belt *(1131 Robson St., ☎ 688-6878)*, though a bit pricey, is a favourite with fashionable teens, but also with those for whom the *look* is paramount.

HMV *(1160 Robson St.)* is the mega-store for music, with great prices on new releases. The store is open late on weekends.

 Tour G: False Creek

Ecomarine Granville Island *(1668 Durenleau St., ☎ 689-7575)* has everything for fans of sea-kayaking. You can even try out the kayaks before you buy.

3 Vets *(2200 Yukon St., ☎ 872-5475)* is a local institution. For 40 years this store has been supplying reasonably priced camping equipment for everyone from professional lumbermen to tree planters and weekend campers.

 Tour H: Shaughnessy and South of Vancouver

Mountain Equipment Co-op *(130 West Broadway, ☎ 872-7858)*. This giant store offers everything you need for your outdoor activities. You must be a member to make purchases; but membership only costs $5.

 Tour I: The Peninsula

Taiga Works *(390 West 8th Ave.)* is a small shop with mountain sports equipment and prices that beat all the competition. Gore-Tex is at half-price. A good address to remember.

Cycling enthusiasts, both off-road and on, should remember **Seymour Bicycle** *(1775 West 4th Ave.,* ☎ *737-9889)*. All the best makes are available, and the staff, who are all cyclists themselves, can provide all sorts of great advice.

UBC Bookstore *(6200 University Boulevard,* ☎ *822-BOOK)* is the largest bookstore west of the Rockies with more than 100,000 titles. Allow enough time to park your car as the parking situation at UBC can be a problem.

Second Suit *(2036 West 4th Ave.,* ☎ *732-0338)* carries the best in formal men's wear from Armani to Boss and Dior.

A stop at **Coast Mountain Sports** *(2201 West 4th Ave.,* ☎ *731-6181)* is *de rigueur* for mountaineers who appreciate quality equipment. Only the best is sold here, and the shop is therefore quite expensive and reserved mostly for pros. The staff are very friendly and experienced.

Leona Lattimer *(1590 West 2nd Ave., west of Granville Island,* ☎ *732-4556)* is a lovely gallery where you can admire some fine native art or if you like, purchase a piece. Quality jewellery and prints. Expensive.

Vegetarian

West Coast

Hotels by Alphabetical Order

INDEX

S + M 291 2 + 5 6

Notes de voyage

Notes de voyage

Notes de voyage

Notes de voyage

Notes de voyage

■ **ULYSSES TRAVEL GUIDES**

☐ Affordable Bed & Breakfasts
   in Québec .... $11.95 CAN
                              $9.95 US
☐ Canada's Maritime
   Provinces............... $24.95 CAN
                             $14.95 US
☐ Dominican Republic
   2nd Edition .... $24.95 CAN
                             $16.95 US
☐ El Salvador............. $22.95 CAN
                             $14.95 US
☐ Guadeloupe........... $24.95 CAN
                             $16.95 US
☐ Honduras .... $24.95 CAN
                             $16.95 US
☐ Martinique.............. $24.95 CAN
                             $16.95 US
☐ Montréal .... $19.95 CAN
                             $13.95 US
☐ Ontario .... $24.95 CAN
                             $14.95 US
☐ Panamá .... $24.95 CAN
                             $16.95 US
☐ Portugal................. $24.95 CAN
                             $16.95 US
☐ Provence -
   Côte d'Azur .... $24.95 CAN
                             $14.95 US
☐ Québec................. $24.95 CAN
                             $14.95 US
☐ Toronto .... $19.95 CAN
                             $13.95 US

☐ Vancouver .... $14.95 CAN
                                $9.95 US
☐ Western Canada....... $24.95 CAN
                             $16.95 US

■ **ULYSSES GREEN ESCAPES**

☐ Hiking in the Northeastern
   United States....... $19.95 CAN
                             $13.95 US
☐ Hiking in Québec ..... $19.95 CAN
                             $13.95 US

■ **ULYSSES DUE SOUTH**

☐ Cartagena (Colombia) . $9.95 CAN
                              $5.95 US
☐ Montelimar (Nicaragua) $9.95 CAN
                              $5.95 US
☐ Puerto Plata - Sosua - Cabarete
   (Dominican Republic) .. $9.95 CAN
                              $5.95 US
☐ St. Barts.................... $9.95 CAN
                              $7.95 US
☐ St. Martin .... $9.95 CAN
                              $7.95 US

■ **ULYSSES TRAVEL JOURNAL**

☐ Ulysses Travel Journal $9.95 CAN
                              $7.95 US

QUANTITY	TITLES	PRICE	TOTAL
	Sub-total		
	Postage & Handling		$4.00
	Sub-total		
	G.S.T.in Canada 7%		
	TOTAL		

NAME:_____

ADDRESS:_____

_____

_____

Payment: ☐ Money Order ☐ Visa ☐ MasterCard
Card Number:_____
Expiry Date:_____
Signature_____

ULYSSES TRAVEL PUBLICATIONS
4176 Rue Saint-Denis, Montréal, Québec, H2W 2M5
☎(514) 843-9447 fax (514) 843-9448